rororo sprachen
Herausgegeben von
Ludwig Moos

Engländer lieben Jokes. Was läge also näher, als Sprechsituationen über Witze meistern zu lernen. Mit "Joke by Joke to Conversation" lernen Sie auf vergnügliche Weise, Kontakte zu knüpfen, Gefühle auszudrücken oder Sorgen und Zweifel zu artikulieren. Sie erwerben Sprechstrategien des Erlaubens, Verbietens, Kritisierens, des Ab- und Zuratens und viele andere mehr. Lockere Tests überprüfen, ob der Lerneffekt gezündet hat, ausführliche Worterklärungen sichern den Lacherfolg.

Dr. René Bosewitz, B. A. (Hons.), der *native speaker* ist, war von 1985 bis 1988 Lektor der englischen Sprache an der Pädagogischen Hochschule Heidelberg und ist gegenwärtig als Examiner of the Chamber of Commerce (London) für English as a Foreign Language und als English Language Consultant in verschiedenen Wirtschaftsunternehmen tätig. Robert Kleinschroth unterrichtet Englisch und Französisch am Gymnasium und leitet die Sprachschule eines Industriebetriebs. Zusammen haben sie in der Reihe 'rororo sprachen' den Band "Joke Your Way Through English Grammar" (8527) veröffentlicht.

CONVERSATION

René Bosewitz
Robert Kleinschroth

Joke by Joke to Conversation

Sprechsituationen mit Witz gemeistert

rororo
Rowohlt

17.–19. Tausend August 1995

Originalausgabe
Veröffentlicht im Rowohlt Taschenbuch Verlag GmbH,
Reinbek bei Hamburg, November 1990

Umschlagillustration Gerd Huss
Umschlagtypographie Peter Wippermann / Nina Rothfos
Kapitelstarter Mathias Hütter
Satz Times (Linotronic 500)
Gesamtherstellung Clausen & Bosse, Leck
Printed in Germany
1290-ISBN 3 499 18797 3

Table of Contents

Inhalt

Vorwort

Aller guten Dinge sind drei. Drei Bücher brauchen wir, um eine Sprache zu lernen. Ein Wörterbuch für Wortschatz und idiomatische Ausdrücke, denn mit Wörtern, Händen, Füßen und Grimassen können wir einige Zeit im fremden Land überleben. Doch bald brauchen wir ein zweites Buch, eine Grammatik, um mit unseren Wörtern Sätze zu bauen. Jetzt sprechen wir das Schulenglisch, mit dem wir Deutsche im internationalen Vergleich nicht schlecht abschneiden.

"Joke by Joke to Conversation" ist ein Buch der dritten Art. Mit mehr als fünfhundert ausgewählten Witzen ist es eine Anthologie des angelsächsischen Humors, aber nicht nur das. Es ist ebenso wichtig und seriös wie Wörterbuch und Grammatik. Es hilft Ihnen mit viel Witz, Ihre Gefühle, Wünsche, Sorgen und Meinungen so zu "verpacken", wie es der gebildete Engländer zu tun pflegt. Sie werden einen Schritt vom Schulenglisch weg hin zur Sprachbeherrschung tun. Um eine Sprechsituation zu meistern, müssen wir zum Beispiel über die sprachlichen Schachzüge und Redemittel, die *speech functions*, verfügen, die es erlauben, Argumente, Vorschläge und Beschwerden wirkungsvoll in das Gespräch einzubringen oder schnell auf sie zu reagieren.

So lernen Sie in diesem Buch unter anderem, partnergerechte Kritik zu üben. Wie sagen Sie Ihrem Ehepartner, Ihrem Vorgesetzten, daß er zuviel Alkohol trinkt? Mit Schulenglisch reicht es für die saft- und kraftlose Feststellung: *"You drink too much alcohol"*. Der fortgeschrittene Leser weiß wahrscheinlich, daß man zumindest die Floskel *"I'm afraid..."* vorausschicken sollte. In diesem Buch lernen Sie, diesen Sachverhalt Ihrem Chauffeur mit den Worten *"Why the hell are you drinking that much, Charles?"* vorzuhalten. Der gute Charles muß umgekehrt, will er seinen Job behalten, unbedingt so formulieren: *"I hope you forgive me for saying so, sir, but shouldn't we drink a cup of coffee for a change."* Die Ehefrau mag denken *"You are a damned alcoholic"*, wird aber, wenn sie klug ist, es erst einmal mit *"Darling! Must you drink that much?"* versuchen.

Neben solchen Sprachkonventionen und Sprechstrategien lernen Sie, wie man seine Haltung und seine Gefühle der Situation und dem Partner gegenüber angemessen zum Ausdruck bringt, wie man sich differenziert und idiomatisch richtig mitteilt. Sie halten also die Kombination aus einem Knigge und einem Ratgeber für englische Sprechsituationen in Händen, Situationen, denen Sie bei der Begegnung mit Engländern nicht ausweichen können.

Heidelberg, Rosenmontag 1990
René Bosewitz
Robert Kleinschroth

Your First Jokes – Your First Test

1. Read this page.
2. If you like it, you are the ideal reader for this book.
3. If you don't like it, please read on. There are more and better jokes for you on the following pages.

* * *

Bob: I'd love you to stay the night, but I'm afraid you'll have to make your own bed.
René: Oh, that's perfectly alright, I don't mind at all.
Bob: Right. Here's a hammer, a saw, and some nails. The wood's in the garage.

* * *

What happens to a girl that goes out with an East-Friesian?
Well, nothing.

* * *

There's nothing wrong with sex on television, just as long as you don't fall off.

* * *

The opening lines of one of the many letters Chancellor Kohl got from people in Dresden:
"Sir,
I never forget a face, but in your case I'll make an exception…"

* * *

"It's a boy," the doctor told Bob. "Eight pounds exactly."
"I'll give you a cheque," stammered Bob.

* * *

Why are elephants big, grey and wrinkled?
If they were small, smooth and white, they would be aspirins.

Gebrauchsanweisung

Warum Witze, Graffiti und humorvolle Zitate? Die Beispiele herkömmlicher Sprachbücher haben einige Nachteile für das Erlernen einer Sprache. Meist sind sie künstlich konstruiert, banal und ohne Zusammenhang. Sie machen deshalb keinen Sinn für den Leser. Sinnlose, zusammenhanglose Sätze aber prägen sich schlecht ein.

Der Witz ist ein kurzer, abgeschlossener Text, der eine Situation schildert oder eine kleine Geschichte in lebendiger Umgangssprache erzählt. Mit diesem Buch lernen Sie Sprache im Kontext, eingebettet in Situationen.

Ferner ist ein Witz mit Pointe eine intellektuelle Herausforderung. Man liest ihn, bis man ihn verstanden hat. Ist der Witz gut, wird man ihn weitererzählen. Kein zusammenhangloser Grammatiksatz motiviert zu diesen Wiederholungen und Anwendungen. Wiederholen und Anwenden ist das A und O des Sprachenlernens.

Und schließlich verhilft uns eine gute Pointe zu einem "Aha-Erlebnis". Deshalb geht ein Witz viel leichter vom Kurzzeitgedächtnis in das Langzeitgedächtnis über als trockene Grammatikbeispiele.

Die Kapitel können unabhängig voneinander gelesen und genossen werden. Dennoch folgt ihre Anordnung einer natürlichen Logik: Sie sprechen einen Engländer an, werden sein Gast und überstehen sprachlich verschiedene Einladungen. Nach näherer Bekanntschaft wird man seine Sorgen teilen, Ratschläge annehmen oder ablehnen, um Gefallen bitten, seine Meinung äußern und schließlich auch einmal Kritik üben.

Nicht nur die einzelnen Kapitel können unabhängig voneinander behandelt werden, die rechten Seiten sind für sich allein eine Anthologie des angelsächsischen Humors. Sie enthalten die Beispiele zu den Sprechfunktionen.

Die linken Seiten sind in ihrer Gesamtheit ein kleines Lexikon der Redemittel. Sie helfen Ihnen, sich schnell auf eine Situation sprachlich vorzubereiten und einzustellen.

Auch wenn Sie nicht über jeden Witz lachen können, sollen Sie doch jeden Witz verstehen. Dafür sorgt das ausführliche Wörterverzeichnis am Ende des Buches.

Eine heitere Testseite am Ende eines jeden Kapitels erlaubt Ihnen, das Gelernte zu überprüfen und zu vertiefen. Die Lösungen der Tests finden Sie im Anhang.

Wir wünschen Ihnen viel Vergnügen.

Extra Fun Page

Bob and Mary had been married for ten years without children. Then one day the doctor told Mary that she was pregnant. Full of joy she rang up Bob at his office.
"Bob! Imagine, I'm pregnant!" There was a long silence. Then Bob stammered: "Who's speaking?"

* * *

A woman brought her husband to court.
"Judge," she said, "I want a divorce. All he thinks about is horses. He talks about nothing else. He isn't interested in me at all. He doesn't even remember the day we got married."
"That's a lie," said the man with a sudden passion showing up in his eyes, "That was the day, when Fury won the race at Ascot."

* * *

When Mrs Margaret Thatcher, Monsieur Mittérand and Herr Kohl met to discuss Germany's future, the German Chancellor said, "I had a dream last night in which I became Chancellor of all of Europe."
"That's funny," said the French President, "I had a similar dream. I became President of the western hemisphere."
And Margaret Thatcher thundered, "Rubbish, I'm not going to appoint you, gentlemen."

* * *

"What do you call a gorilla with a machine gun?" – "Sir!"

* * *

Since the official paper of the Vatican, the Osservatore Romano, announced that there were 1166 sins possible under the Catholic law their office has been swamped with enquiries from all over the world asking for the complete list.

Starting And Ending Conversations
Sprachliches An- und Abbandeln

Stellen Sie sich vor, Sie stehen mitten in der Millionenstadt London, und keiner redet mit Ihnen. Ach, so ergeht es Ihnen im Ausland auch manchmal? Dabei würden wir so gerne mit unseren Sprachkenntnissen glänzen und diese im Gespräch mit einem *native speaker* verbessern. Da haben wir Mann beziehungsweise Frau zu Hause gelassen – und kommen in Hotel und Sprachschule immer nur mit Landsleuten ins Gespräch. Zufall? Schicksal? Mit diesen *conversation openers* wird das nicht mehr passieren.

Sprachliches An- und Abbandeln

1. Gesprächsanbahnung

Nutzen Sie das Gelände und die Situation! Stellen Sie harmlose Fragen! Bieten Sie Ihre Dienste an!

Excuse me for mentioning it, but …
Excuse me, *is this seat taken?*
Nice place. ***Do you come here often?***
I beg your pardon. *Was that your foot / glass / chair?*
You look a bit lost. ***Can I help you?***
I beg your pardon, but *are you John Doorbar?*
Can I get you a drink? *What are you drinking?*
You look worried. ***Can I help you?***

Annahme von Angeboten	Ablehnung von Angeboten
Yes, of course. / Sure.	***I'd like to say yes, but…***
I'd be glad to.	***I can't really because…***
By all means.	***I'm awfully sorry, but…***

Banale Bemerkungen über das Wetter lockern auch dem schweigsamsten Angelsachsen die Zunge:

Nasty weather, isn't it?
Been raining like this for long, has it?

Schaffen Sie Gemeinsamkeit! Machen Sie ihn zum Leidensgefährten!

It's rather *hot / cold / crowded in here,* ***don't you think?***
What a *slow bus / dirty place* ***it is!***

Starting And Ending Conversations

A penguin enters a pub and orders a pint of beer. He puts a fiver on the bar and the barman gives him £1 change. The penguin drinks up and starts to leave.
"**Excuse me for mentioning it**," says the astonished barman, "but we don't get many penguins in here."
"I'm not surprised," answers the penguin, "with beer at £4 a pint."

* * *

A man took his pet to an animal auction. A German tourist, who had already studied this chapter, plucked up his courage and said:
"**Excuse me, but** that's a very strange dog you have there. What sort is it?"
"It's a long-nosed, long-tailed, sharp-toothed terrier", replied the man. "Some people also call them alligators."

* * *

"**Er... Umm.. Excuse me, but** would you like to dine out with me tonight?"
"**I'd like to say yes, but** I never go out with perfect strangers."
"Who said I was perfect?"

* * *

Bob: **Excuse me, may I ask you a question**? I know it's not my business, but why are you jumping up and down like that?
René: Because I've just taken some medicine and I forgot to shake the bottle.

* * *

The absent-minded professor got up from the table in the restaurant and took an overcoat from the stand and put it on. Then a man walked up to him and said: "**I beg your pardon, but** are you Mr John Doorbar?"
"No," said the professor, "I'm afraid not."
"Well, I am," said the man, "and that's John Doorbar's coat you are putting on."

2. Gesprächspflege

Nun treten Sie aus der Anonymität heraus und stellen sich vor:

By the way, *my name is Meier. I am from Gelsenkirchen.*

Erzählen Sie aber Ihre Lebensgeschichte nicht in einem Stück:

I'm here on a holiday/business trip/for the first time.

Wenn Sie immer noch nicht ins Gespräch kommen, dann war ihr Gegenüber eben kein Engländer, sondern Österreicher. Wie wär's mit Ihrer Nachbarin?

3. Das Wort abschneiden oder das Thema wechseln

Die Lebensgeschichte Ihrer Nachbarin verliert an Faszination. Sie möchten nun von Ihrer Briefmarkensammlung erzählen. Das geht so:

If I might interrupt you for a moment...
May I interrupt you for a moment?
Sorry to interrupt, but...
I'd just like to say that...
I don't want to interrupt you, but...
Could I just...?
Hang on,...
Oh, I've just noticed something.

Starting And Ending Conversations

René's favourite conversation opener:
"**By the way, my name is**... Oh, forget it, I'm glad you don't recognize me. I'd rather have you like me for myself."

* * *

How to switch on a rare beauty:
"You can't be real. May I pinch you to see if I'm dreaming? **By the way, my name is** Meier. I'm here on a business trip."

* * *

After their luxury liner had sunk in a violent storm, two friends found themselves shipwrecked on a small island in the Pacific. On the morning of the third day one of them sank to his knees and began to pray. "Oh Lord, I know I'm a miserable sinner, but if you save us now I'll change my ways. I'll go to church every Sunday, I'll be good to my wife, I'll give up drinking and gambling. I'll stop..." – "**I don't want to interrupt you**," said his friend, "**but** I wouldn't go too far. I think I can see a ship coming."

* * *

Young man:	How about a drive in the country?
Pretty girl:	Will there be any kissing... and cuddling and... parking in lonely lanes and...?
Young man:	**I'd just like to say that** you can be sure nothing of that sort will happen.
Pretty girl:	Oh, then what are we going for?

* * *

"Mummy", said little Bobby, "I want to live with Bridget next door." "But you're only six years old," smiled his mother. "Where will you live?" – "In her bedroom, of course and we..." – "**Hey, hang on a minute**", interrupted his mother. "What will you do if little babies come along?" – "Well," said Bobby seriously, "we've been alright so far... and if she lays any eggs I'll tread on them."

4. Sprachliche Ellenbogen in Konferenzen und Diskussionen

Als rhetorisch geschulter Manager schneiden Sie Gesprächsfäden ab, während der andere Atem schöpft. Mit gut geheucheltem Interesse knüpfen Sie an seine letzte Bemerkung an, um das Wort zu ergreifen und zu behalten.

How fascinating! That reminds me of…
By the way, I've just remembered…

In Konferenzen trägt man wie folgt zur Verfeinerung der Gesprächskultur bei:

Could I break in a moment here?
Could I come in at this point?
If I could just say a few words here.

Als Vorgesetzter oder *chairperson* erwehren Sie sich der Verbesserungsvorschläge karrierebewußter Mitarbeiter mit dem Wortschatz, der Ihrer Stellung den rechten Ausdruck verleiht:

Perhaps we should move on to the next point.
If nobody has anything to add I'd like to draw the meeting to an end.
I think we should call it a day.
Well gentlemen, that's enough for today.
Let's have a vote and wrap up the meeting.

Starting And Ending Conversations

A group of German tourists was visiting a castle in Scotland. The lord, a handsome young man wearing a kilt, was boring his audience to death with endless explanations about Gothic architecture. Finally a pretty girl who could not stand this any longer interrupted his monologue:
“**By the way, I’ve just remembered** what I wanted to ask. What is worn under your kilt?”
With a fine smile the Scotsman replied: “Nothing is *worn*, my dear. Everything is in perfect working condition.”
(wear, wore, worn = tragen und abnutzen)

* * *

The executives of an opinion poll company were busy discussing whether sex was pleasure or hard work. “It’s the best thing in life, and if you allow me to...” – “**If I could just make a point here**,” interrupted another, “You wait till you are married. After a year it becomes a chore like everything else. Let me give you an example...” – “**If I could just say a few words here**,” interrupted a third, “we are all too intellectual. Let us ask our new office boy”. A decision was made. “Tell us,” they asked him, “is sex work or pleasure?” The young man thought for a moment, then he replied: “It must be a pleasure, because if it was work, you’d be making me do it for you.”

* * *

The managing director of a small company ruled all parts of his enterprise with a rod of iron. At the end of a particularly long and stormy management meeting he finally looked round the boardroom table and said: “Okay! **Let’s have a vote and call it a day**. All who don’t share my opinion raise their hands and say ‘I resign’.”

Test
Starting And Ending Conversations

1. Choose the most appropriate response.

At Frankfurt Airport

Man: Excuse me, you look worried. Can I help you?

Woman: Oh, that's very nice of you. Actually I'm in a terrible hurry. My plane leaves in twenty minutes and I can't find hall B. Perhaps you could tell me how to get there.

Man: __________You are standing in it.

a) By the way, *b) I beg your pardon?*
c) I'm awfully sorry. *d) By all means.*

2. Match up the sentences in the two columns.

René says:	Robert replies:
1. It's rather cold in here.	a) Oh, I didn't realise.
2. Sorry to interrupt but I think you are in the wrong place.	b) Sure I do.
3. By the way do you know her?	c) Oh, I'm awfully sorry.
4. You can't do that in here.	d) Somebody has left the door open.
5. Well, that's it for today.	e) Sure is.

3. Give the most appropriate function for the German in the brackets.

TV interviewer: Well, just one last question and *(wir können dieses Interview beenden)*. On a lighter note Mrs. Thatcher, have you heard the latest political jokes?

Mrs Thatcher: Heard them? I appointed them all.

4. What would you say if...

You were leading a discussion. You're all tired and want to go home?

a) Could I break in a moment? *b) I'm awfully sorry.*
c) I've just remarked something. *d) I think we should call it a day.*

How Are You?

Wie geht es Ihnen?

Über das Wetter spricht der Engländer gerne überall und mit jedem. Spricht er mit Ihnen aber über das zweite Universalthema, die Gesundheit, dann dürfen Sie sich zu seinem weiteren Bekanntenkreis zählen.

Wie geht es Ihnen?

1. Die Frage nach dem Wohlbefinden als Gruß

Die Frage ***How are you***? ist weniger eine Frage nach dem Wohlbefinden als ein Gruß*. Sie sollte bei entfernten Bekannten mit einer Variante von ***Fine, thank you*** beantwortet werden, ganz gleich, wie miserabel man sich fühlt. Mit der Gegenfrage ***And how are you***? wird das Gegenüber zu einer ähnlichen Notlüge aufgefordert.

	Fine, thank you.
	Oh, not bad.
How are you?	***It could be worse.***
	I can't complain.
	I've nothing to complain about.

Weitere Fragen und Antworten (von Menschen, die gesund sein wollen). Beide sind fast beliebig kombinierbar:

Frage	Antwort
How are you this morning?	***I'm feeling great.***
How are you these days?	***I feel on top of the world.***
How are things with you today?	***Not too bad, thanks.***
How is it going?	***I couldn't feel better.***
How's life been treating you?	***I'm in the best of health.***
How do you find life nowadays?	***I'm getting on nicely.***
How are you keeping nowadays?	***Well, I'm as fit as a fiddle.***

* Auch ***How do you do***? ist wider Erwarten keine Frage, sondern ein Gruß, den man ebenfalls mit ***How do you do***? erwidert.

How Are You?

Astronaut Gordon Cooper was about to start on his memorable flight into space when one of the reporters approached him and asked: "**How do you feel**?"
Cooper replied, "**I feel miserable**. I'm worried."
The reporter said, "Why should you be worried when you think of what you are doing for your country?"
Cooper then said, "I've got to remember every one of these gadgets in this machine. There are one thousand gadgets in this rocket and each has been made by the lowest bidder."

* * *

An Irish businessman went to see his doctor about his sexual problems.
"You have been working too hard. Get some exercise," the doctor advised. "Try riding a bike a few miles every day."
Two days later, the doctor received a telephone call from the man.
"**How are you this morning**? Has your sex life improved?" he asked.
"How would I know? I'm seventy miles from home at the moment", was the angry reply.

* * *

Young nurse: Good morning, sir. **How are we this morning**?
Patient: **I feel rotten**. Tell me the truth, Nurse. **What's wrong with me**?
Young nurse: To tell you the truth, I heard one of the doctors say that you've got only a couple of minutes to live.
Patient: Nurse, is there anything you can do for me?
Young nurse: I'm sorry, sir, there isn't much I can do. Perhaps boil an egg.

Wie geht es Ihnen?

2. Besorgte Fragen nach dem Wohlbefinden

Mit folgenden Fragen lassen Sie sich unter Umständen auf ein längeres medizinisches Fachgespräch ein. Falls Sie es eilig haben, sollten Sie beim flüchtigen *How are you*? bleiben.

What's the matter with you?
Are you alright?
Anything wrong with you?
Aren't you feeling well?
It's nothing serious, I hope?
Are you sure you are okay?
How's your leg / headache / flu?

Mit folgenden Antworten vermeiden Sie, Ihre eigene Krankengeschichte erzählen zu müssen, und gestatten dem Gesprächspartner, zu anderen konventionellen Themen überzugehen.

It could be worse.
I feel a bit run down.
I've felt better.
It's almost alright now.
(I feel) pretty much the same as always.
I'm over the worst.

How Are You?

Doctor: **How are you today?**
Bob: **Pretty much the same.** I keep losing my memory.
Doctor: When did that start?
Bob: When did what start?

* * *

McGregor went to see his doctor for a medical check-up. As requested by the doctor, he took along a specimen of urine in an unusually big bottle. After the test, he rushed home. "**Everything alright**?" his wife wanted to know. "Good news, Anne. You, Aunt Mary, the kids and the dog, **we are all in perfect shape**."

* * *

René: **How's your leg today?**
Bob: I went to see the specialist about it.
René: What did he say?
Bob: **Could be worse.** He said **he would have me back on my feet** in a fortnight.
René: And did he?
Bob: Yes – I had to sell the car to pay him.

* * *

"And how is your poor husband?"
"Thank you, much better. Yesterday he was enjoying poor health, today he's complaining of feeling better."

* * *

McTavish had a brainstorm and bought two two-penny tickets in a raffle. He won £1000.
"**How do you feel** after your big win?" asked McNab.
"Disappointed," said McTavish. "My other ticket didn't win anything."

* * *

René: **How's your insomnia**?
Bob: **Worse**. I can't even sleep when it's time to get up.

Wie geht es Ihnen?

3. Besorgte Feststellungen – Mögliche pessimistische Reaktionen

Mit folgenden Beobachtungen gehe man in den ersten Tagen der Bekanntschaft noch sparsam um. Bei Hypochondern allerdings können Sie gar nicht oft genug davon Gebrauch machen.

Feststellung	Reaktion
You look like the shadow of your former self.	*Well, I could do with a holiday.*
You look a bit tired.	*Yes, I don't feel well at all.*
You look pale today.	*Actually, I feel awful.*
You don't look so well.	*I feel a bit run down.*
You're looking a bit down in the mouth.	*I'm just a little tired.*
You don't look so good today.	*I'm not feeling so good.*
You look as if you should be in bed.	*I feel rotten / lousy.*
You really look under the weather.	*Well, I'm afraid I must see the doctor.*
I don't like the looks of you.	*I've got a cold.*
I've seen you look better.	*I'm afraid I've got the flu.*
You look a bit the worse for the wear.	*Well, I'm not feeling so good.*
	I'm afraid I'm on my last legs.

* * *

A drunk went to the doctor. "Doctor, ***I'm afraid my health is not too good. I've got a headache and my stomach is completely upset.***
After a thorough check-up the doctor said: "Hmm, you will have to give up certain things."
"What sort of things?"
"Well, wine and women for a start. But you can sing as much as you want."

How Are You?

Bob: **You look like the shadow of your former self. Anything wrong with you?**

René: **I don't feel well at all.** I keep seeing pink mice every time I try to go to sleep.

Bob: Have you seen a psychiatrist?

René: No, only pink mice.

* * *

Doctor: **I don't like the looks** of your husband.

Wife: I don't either. But he's good to the children.

* * *

Bob: Hello old boy. My God, **you do look tired**!

René: Well, I'm getting old. Nowadays it takes me all night to do what I used to do all night.

* * *

Doctor: **You look as if you should be in bed.**

Michael: Well, doctor, **I've been feeling terrible** all week.

Doctor: Well, get undressed and I'll examine you.

Twenty minutes later:

Doctor: Sorry, but I can't find anything wrong with you. It might be the alcohol.

Michael: OK – I'll come back when you're sober.

* * *

Bob: **I don't like the looks of you, old man. Anything wrong?**

René: **And I feel bad, too.** As a matter of fact, **I have been feeling awful for the last four weeks.** I've got a temperature, a splitting headache, a heart condition.... well, to cut a long story short, I think, hypochondria is the only disease I haven't got.

* * *

Wife to sick McNab: Poor dear, I'm going to ring for the doctor. **You look awful.**

McNab: Make it the undertaker. I can't afford a middleman.

Test
How Are You?

1. Choose the most appropriate response.

Bob: Hi Neil. _______________?

Neal: Well, except for the fact that my girlfriend left me, I'm overweight, I've got financial problems and I've lost my job, I'm feeling fine.

Bob: Nothing new then?

a) *How are you?*

b) *Are you feeling well?*

c) *How's life been treating you?*

d) *You look a bit the worse for wear.*

2. Fit in an appropriate function or phrase.

Ronny: Anything wrong with you? _______________

Bob: Well, it's my psychiatrist. I finally managed to have an orgasm... and he told me it was the wrong kind.

3. Match up the sentences in the two columns.

René says:	Robert replies:
1. Aren't you feeling well?	a) I'm feeling a bit depressed.
2. How are you these days?	b) Yes, I reckon I have to see a doctor.
3. You're looking a bit down in the mouth.	c) Alright, thanks.
4. I don't like the looks of you.	d) I'm getting on nicely.
5. How are you?	e) No, I've got stomach trouble.

4. Give the most appropriate function for the German in the brackets.

Bob: Doctor, doctor, *(mit meinen Augen stimmt was nicht)*.

Doctor: You certainly have, sir. This is a butcher's shop.

Inviting And Being Invited

Kleiner Knigge für Gast und Gastgeber

Nach dem erfolgreichen Einsatz der Redemittel des sprachlichen Anbandelns geraten Sie unweigerlich in die erste Standardsituation: Sie werden eingeladen. Um nicht sprachloses Opfer britischer Gastfreundschaft zu werden, erhalten Sie hier das unentbehrliche Rüstzeug, das Ihnen erlaubt, Einladungen nach Art des Landes abzulehnen oder anzunehmen und am konventionellen Partygespräch teilzunehmen.

Knigge für Gast und Gastgeber

1. Einladung und dankende Annahme

Die folgenden Einladungen sind nach dem zunehmenden Grad der Höflichkeit und Förmlichkeit angeordnet. Die Formen des Dankes sind fast alle austauschbar:

Einladung	Annahme
How about a beer at my place?	***Thanks very much.***
Why not have a drink?	***Good idea.***
Why not join us?	***Thanks a lot.***
Won't you join us for...?	***I'd love to.***
Why don't you join us?	***Thanks for inviting me.***
Will you join us for lunch?	***I'd like to very much.***
You could join us if you want.	***Yes, with pleasure.***
How about coming for lunch tomorrow?	***That would be nice.***
Would you like to come for tea?	***Thank you. That's very kind of you.***
How would you like to dine with us?	

Mit dem Gewicht des Anlasses nimmt der sprachliche Aufwand zu:

May I invite you to *our house-warming party?*
I'd like to invite you to *my daughter's wedding.*
I was wondering if you'd care to *come to our concert?*
I was wondering if you'd fancy *having dinner with us?*
We would be pleased if you would honour us with your company on the occasion of....

Inviting And Being Invited

My wife was complaining about me going out night after night. So, one day I said: "**Well, why don't you join me**, for once?" – "**Good idea**!" she agreed. At the pub, I said to her: "**Now, how about a drink? Would you like to try a whisky?**" I ordered her a whisky; she took one mouthful and spat it out. "I don't know how you can drink this stuff. It tastes awful." – "There you are," I cried, "and you think I'm out enjoying myself all the time."

* * *

"**I wonder if you would care to** come to my house-warming party on Saturday, Ronny?"
"**Thank you. That's very nice of you**. Where do you live?"
"Number 32, Wilton Crescent. Just push the bell with your nose."
"Why with my nose?"
"You're not coming empty-handed, are you?"

* * *

The professor was giving the last lecture of the term. "The examination papers are already in the hands of the printer," he concluded. "**Now I'd like to invite you to** ask any questions you might consider important." – Silence, then a weak voice: "Who's the printer?"

* * *

Patient: Doctor, I'm going to be bald. I don't want to lose my hair. What can you give me?
Doctor: **What would you like?** A cigar box or a brown paper bag?

* * *

A tramp decided he would shame McTavish into giving him some money, so he went down on his hands and knees and began to eat the grass in McTavish's front garden. The old miser stuck his head out of the window and asked the tramp what he was doing there. "I'm eating the grass," said the tramp, "because I'm starving." – "**Come on in,**" said McTavish. "**I wonder if you'd like to have lunch** in my back garden. The grass there is much longer."

Knigge für Gast und Gastgeber

2. Die Redemittel häuslicher Gastfreundschaft

Vom Klingeln an der Haustür bis zum ersten Drink fallen mit einiger Sicherheit folgende unvermeidliche Worte:

Come in! Do come in! Won't you come in?
It's good to see you here again.
Have a seat! Do sit down! Make yourself at home!
Can I get you a drink? Help yourself to a drink. Help yourself to some more.
How about some more?
Can I offer you a drink? Would you like a sherry?

3. Die Strategien des "Sich-Verabschiedens"

Wer sich nicht auf französisch verabschiedet, muß sich einem kleinen sprachlichen Ritual unterziehen:

Den Aufbruch ankündigen	Einen Grund angeben
I'm afraid I've got to leave. *I'm afraid I must be going now.* *I really can't stay any longer.* *I think I should be going now.*	*I've got a train to catch.* *Tomorrow is going to be a hard day for me.* *I don't want to overstay my welcome.*

Der Gastgeber drückt sein Bedauern aus
I'm sorry you can't stay a bit longer. *It's a pity you can't stay.*

Inviting And Being Invited

“**Come on in, Bob,**” said the lady to the postman hesitating at the gate. “That’s a fierce dog you’ve got,” said Bob nervously, pointing to the enormous dog barking furiously at him.
“Don’t you know a barking dog never bites?” said the lady.
“Sure I know it,” said Bob. “What I’m wondering is, does the dog know it?”

* * *

Host: **May I offer you something to drink**?
Guest: A glass of *vin rouge* would be fine.
Host: **Certainly.** Red or white?
Guest: I don’t care. I’m colour-blind.

* * *

Shortly after the plane took off, the passengers heard a soft and comforting voice through the loudspeaker: “Welcome on board our completely automatic supersonic airliner. **We are happy to have you with us. Please sit down. Make yourselves comfortable and help yourselves to** drinks from your computerized bar. This plane is completely automatic: automatic pilot, automatic services, automatic starting and landing devices. Absolutely nothing can go wrong ... go wrong ... go wr ... go wr ... go ... go ...”

* * *

René: Would you like a lemon with your tea?
Bob: No, I prefer to be alone.

* * *

First Bavarian: I say, my wife read *Double Trouble* and then she had twins.
Second Bavarian: That’s nothing, my wife read *The Three Musketeers* and then she had triplets.
Third Bavarian: **I’m afraid I’ve got to be going now.** I left the wife reading *Ali Baba And The Forty Thieves*.

Knigge für Gast und Gastgeber

4. Wie man sich für einen Abend bedankt

An der Haustür sollte sich unter gebildeten Menschen eine Variante dieser Szene abspielen:

Gast:	Sich für die Einladung bedanken
Gastgeber:	Auf den Dank reagieren
Guest:	***Thank you ever so much. This has been a most pleasant evening.***
Host:	***We're looking forward to having you with us again.***
Guest:	***Thank you so much for the superb dinner.***
Host:	***It was our pleasure.***
Guest:	***I'd like to thank you most sincerely.***
Host:	***Don't mention it! I hope you enjoyed yourself.***
Guest:	***Well, the whole evening was really enjoyable.***
Host:	***It's been a pleasure. May I show you out?***
Guest:	***I'd like to express my thanks for a most wonderful evening.***
Host:	***Not at all. Can I see you home, perhaps?***

Wer Geselligkeit und lange Abende scheut, benötigt die Strategien des "Nein-Sagens", vorgestellt auf der übernächsten Seite: Wie man Einladungen ablehnt.

Inviting And Being Invited

Guest: **I'm afraid I've got to leave now. I'd like to thank you for this wonderful evening. Don't trouble to show me out.**
Host: **It's no trouble. It will be a pleasure.**

* * *

George Bernard Shaw sent Churchill two tickets for his new play:
"**I would be pleased if you would honour me with your company on the occasion of the opening night of my new play.**
P. S. And bring a friend, if you have one."

Churchill wrote to Shaw the following lines:
"**I'd like to thank you most sincerely for the tickets. I very much regret that I'm otherwise engaged on that evening.** Please send two tickets for the second performance, if there is one."

* * *

It was the first time that we took our ten-year-old Linda to a dinner party which the wife of my boss had invited us to. When it was time to leave I told her to thank our hostess.
"Say, **I'd like to thank you for a most wonderful evening**."
At home I asked Linda if she had said thank-you to our hostess.
"No, I didn't," she said.
"Why not?" I wanted to know.
"Well, a lady in front of me wanted to thank her, but she said '**Don't mention it**', so I didn't."

* * *

Bob: **Thank you for this extraordinary evening.**
René: **Don't mention it. I hope you enjoyed yourself.**
Bob: Yes, I did, since there was nothing else to enjoy.

Knigge für Gast und Gastgeber

5. Wie man Einladungen ablehnt

Die Skala der Ablehnungen reicht von unhöflich bis sehr höflich. Es ist üblich, den Grund des Fernbleibens anzugeben.

No, it's not my cup of tea.
No, I'd rather not.
I'm sorry, *I don't have time.*

I'm afraid I've got a previous appointment.
I'd like to but I've got *a bad flu.*
Thank you for asking me but…
Thank you. I'd love to but…
I'd have enjoyed it but…
I very much regret that I can't…
I'd have been very glad to, but…

Auf eine höfliche Ablehnung reagiert man so:

Well, it can't be helped, I suppose.
What a pity!
Well, that's a pity.
It would have been fun.
Well then, some other time perhaps.

Inviting And Being Invited

Lady Astor wrote to George Bernard Shaw the following letter of invitation: "**My husband and I would like to invite you** to my fortieth birthday. **We are looking forward to seeing you** again after all this time."
The famous author wrote back: "**I very much regret that I won't be able to come** to your fortieth birthday. But I can't tell you how much I enjoyed that same party five years ago."

* * *

Having described all the pleasures of Paradise, the vicar asked the children: "Hands up all who want to go there?" All the children put their hands up except for Susan. "Susan," asked the vicar, "**why don't you want to join me** and your friends in Paradise?" – "**Thank you**," replied Susan, "**I'd have enjoyed it but** my mum said I had to come straight home after church."

* * *

Bobby: We've got a new dog. **Would you like to come and** play with him?
Ronny: **Thank you, I'd love to but** I've heard him barking and growling. He sounds very unfriendly. Does he bite?
Bobby: That's what I'd like to find out.

* * *

"**Can I get you a drink?**" I asked the most stunning looking girl at the otherwise rather dull party. "**No thank you. I'd rather not.**" – "**How about a cigarette?**" – "**No, thank you.** I don't smoke." she replied. "Then, **why not join me for** a game of darts?" I suggested. – "**I don't want to seem rude, but I'm afraid** I don't play." – I made a last effort: "Then, **could I perhaps see you home**?" – "**Very well**," she agreed. So we arrived at an elegant house and she opened the door – and there, lying in the hall, was a dead tiger. "Well", she said conscious of my bewilderment, "I never said I was tidy, did I?"

Test
Inviting And Being Invited

1. Choose the most appropriate response.

John: Hey, there's a squash championship next Saturday. I've got a spare ticket. Why not come with us to Frankfurt? We could make a day of it.

Glen: I'd like to go, John, but ____________. I'm more of a family man. And Saturday is the day for the family.

John: Okay. Well, that's a pity. Never mind. See you then.

a) it's not my cup of tea. *b) thanks a lot.*
a) I'd like to but I've got bad flu. *d) some other time, perhaps.*

2. Match up the sentences in the two columns.

René says:	Robert replies:
1. How about coming for an Indian meal tomorrow?	a) Good idea!
2. Why don't we write another book together?	b) Likewise.
3. It's good to see you here again?	c) Thanks but I'm teetotal.
4. Can I get you a sherry?	d) Oh, sorry to hear that.
5. I'm afraid I must be going now.	e) That would be very nice.

3. Give the most appropriate function for the German in the brackets.

Sign in a pub toilet.
"*(Warum benutzen Sie nicht)* the toilet brush?"
Someone had written beneath it:
"Thank you. I tried it but now I've gone back to using toilet paper."

4. What would you say if...

somebody had invited you to stay longer after a dinner at their house but you feel you have been there too long already?

a) I'm sorry. I don't have time. *b) I'd like to but I've got bad flu.*
c) I don't want to overstay my welcome. *d) Sorry, it's not my cup of tea.*

The Right Word At The Right Time

Das rechte Wort zur rechten Zeit

Für gesellschaftliches und geschäftliches Vorankommen im Ausland ist menschliche Kontaktpflege die Wiege des Erfolges. Doch leider werden wir immer wieder Zeuge, wie selbst hochrangige Politiker, von ihrem Schulenglisch im Stich gelassen, auf dem glatten Parkett gesellschaftlicher Ereignisse straucheln. Damit Sie in Gesellschaft brillieren können, sorgen wir für die sprachliche Grundausstattung, auch *small talk* genannt, zu gesellschaftlichen Standardsituationen.

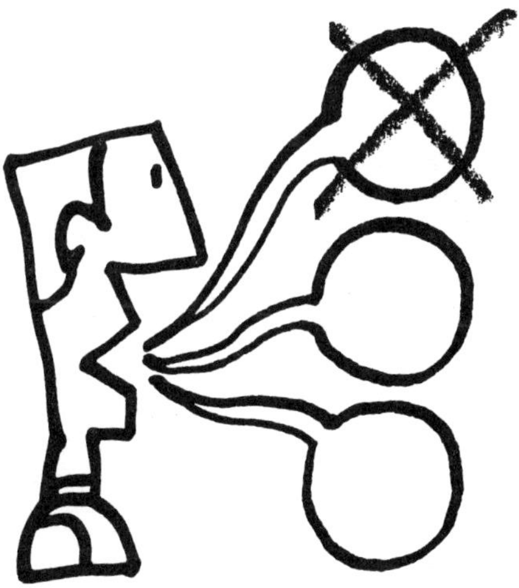

Das rechte Wort zur rechten Zeit

1. Wie macht man Komplimente?

Verlegenes Schweigen kann besonders am Anfang einer Beziehung schon deren Ende sein. Komplimente über Essen, Kleidung, Wohnung, Regierung und andere soziale Errungenschaften hingegen sind die erprobten Eisbrecher.

That was really good!
Delicious! Excellent!
It's out of this world.
I like *your shirt.*
I quite fancy *your hat.*
How *clever* ***you are!***
I must say *you certainly know what's what.*
That's second to none.
It couldn't be better.
I've heard a lot about…
It's unique.
That's a nice *dress.*
You're really charming.
What a beautiful *garden* ***you have.***
I'd like to compliment you on *your success.*
That's a touch of perfection.

2. Der Glückwunsch zum Erfolg

Auch unbedeutende Leistungen Ihrer Gastgeber dürfen Sie nicht schweigend übergehen. Mit den Redemitteln des Lobens und Beglückwünschens finden Sie den Weg zum Herzen jedes Briten.

That's not bad!
Very good!
Well done!
Full marks!
That's great / terrific!
That's absolutely superb!
Not bad at all!
Fine!
That's it!
Good for you!
That's smashing!
That's unique!

I hadn't expected such a good…
Well, that was bang on!

The Right Word At The Right Time

Bob: **I really like your** suit. It fits you like a glove.
René: That's the trouble. It should fit me like a suit.

* * *

She: **I've heard a lot** about your love-making.
He: Oh, it's not worth talking about.
She: Yes, that's what I've heard.

* * *

One doctor to another: **I've heard so much about you**! Now I'd like to hear your side of the story.

* * *

Someone you like is wearing an ugly hat, and she asks you to give her your honest opinion about it:
"**What a lovely hat!** Could I possibly make just one suggestion. If it blows off, don't chase it."

* * *

The boss leaned over his secretary, who was busily painting her fingernails, and said: "Mrs Sutter, **I'd like to compliment you on** your work – but when are you going to do any?"

* * *

At an evening party the hostess coaxed a protesting guest to sing. After the song, she went up to him and said with a smile: "Oh, dear Mr Jenkins, **you must never again tell me that you can't** sing. I know it now."

* * *

A lady on a luxury cruise went down to the galley and said to the head chef, "**I must compliment you** on your excellent Beef Bourguignon! I wonder if I might have the recipe?"
"Certainly, madam," said the chef. "First you take three-thousand onions..."

Das rechte Wort zur rechten Zeit

3. Worte für Glücks-, Krankheits- und Trauerfälle

Bei wichtigen Ereignissen des Kirchenjahres darf man auch als Ausländer nicht sprachlos sein. Doch sind es vor allem die Anlässe, die in keinem Kalender stehen und auf die man sich deshalb auch nicht vorbereiten kann, zu denen der Brite einen Wortbeitrag von Ihnen erwartet.

Prüfungen:	***Well done in your exam.***
Geburtstag:	***Many happy returns!***
	I wish you a happy birthday.
Weihnachten:	***Merry Christmas!***
Neujahr:	***A Happy New Year!***
Hochzeit:	***We wish you all the best.***
Krankheit:	***I wish you a speedy recovery.***

* * *

"I wish you a very happy birthday. May you live to be a hundred *– and then decide if you want to go on."*

The Right Word At The Right Time

Three men were in the hospital waiting-room when the nurse came from the maternity ward. She said to the first man, "**Congratulations,** you're the father of twins. **Well done!**" – "Wonderful," he exclaimed. "Isn't that a coincidence? I'm a member of the Minnesota Twins baseball team."

Later the nurse returned and said to the second man, "**Congratulations,** you're the father of triplets. **Full marks!**"

"Wow," the new father said, "another coincidence. I work for the 3 M Company."

The third man said, "Please excuse me, Nurse, while I get a tranquilizer. I work for the 7-Up Company."

* * *

Samuel and Rachel had been married for fifteen years without children. Then one day, the doctor told Rachel that she was expecting a baby. Excitedly she rang up Samuel at his office. "Samuel, imagine, I'm pregnant."

"**Congratulations**...," then a long silence, then Samuel: "I beg your pardon, who's speaking?"

* * *

Staggering into a bar, a drunk shouted "**Happy New Year, everyone**!" A chap next to him said: "You idiot – it's the middle of June."

"My God," said the drunk, "the wife 'll kill me. I've never been this late before!"

* * *

BEST WISHES FOR A HAPPY AND SUCCESSFUL FIRST MARRIAGE.

* * *

The British Prime Minister, recovering in a London hospital, received this telegram from the Speaker of the House of Commons:

Dear Prime Minister,

the Members of the House **wish you a speedy recovery**... by a vote of 356 to 297.

Das rechte Wort zur rechten Zeit

4. Trauerfälle[1)]

Please accept my deepest sympathy.
I don't know what to say.
It's a great loss to all of us.
I'm so sorry to hear about your husband's death.

1. *Anmerkung*: Der Witz ist eine uralte Form der Auseinandersetzung des Menschen mit seinem Schicksal. Im Witz versucht er, die Gedanken an Krankheit und Tod erträglicher zu machen. Wer daran Anstoß nimmt, möge diese Witze überblättern.

The Right Word At The Right Time

"My wife says she will leave me if I don't throw out my computer."
"**Oh, I'm sorry.**"
"So am I. I'll miss her."

* * *

Antonio's young, beautiful wife dies. At the funeral he is broken-hearted, sobbing and will not leave the grave. His best friend puts his arm around him, "**Please accept my deepest sympathy. I know how you feel**. It was tragic. But think, Antonio, in a few months you'll be singing and dancing again and you'll meet nice girls, you'll marry again and have children. I know your wife would have wanted it."
Antonio raises his tear-stricken face. "You're right! You're right! But... but what am I going to do tonight?"

* * *

"**I was so sorry to hear that your wife died,**" McTavish sympathized with McNab.
"You're not nearly as sorry as I am," replied McNab. "She had taken hardly any of those expensive pills I bought her."

* * *

The priest was visiting the old lady whose husband had died. "**I'm sorry to hear that Joe has passed away. Please accept my deepest sympathy**. He was such a good Christian that he must be in HEAVEN by now. It's a pity we will never see him again."

* * *

"**Please accept my deepest sympathy**," said the vicar to McNab's widow. "**His passing away is a great loss to all of us.** Talking about loss, a funeral service with 20 candles costs about £ 100, with 10 candles £ 60 and with 5 candles... hm... £ 30, but believe me, that would be no fun."

Das rechte Wort zur rechten Zeit

5. Vorstellung, Begrüßung und Verabschiedung

Die erste Begegnung	
A: Mr Pitt, ***may I introduce you to Mrs*** *Bell.* ***This is Mr*** *Pritt.*	
B: ***How do you do? My name is*** *Mary Bell.*	
A: Paul, ***I'd like you to meet*** *Peter. Peter,* ***this is*** *Paul.*	
B: How do you do?	
C: ***How do you do?***	
A: Paul, ***have you met*** *Peter? Peter,* ***this is*** *Paul.*	
B: ***Pleased to meet you.***	*informell:* ***Hi.***
C: ***The pleasure is mine.***	*informell:* ***Hi.***

Die zweite und weitere Begegnungen
"Hello *Peter.* ***How are you?"*** –
"Hello, *Paul.* ***Fine, thank you. And how are you?"***
"Is that you, *Paul?* ***I haven't seen you for ages."***
"How is life? / How has life been treating you since we last met?"

Sollten die Gastgeber der Party Sie vergessen haben, spielen Sie nicht das Mauerblümchen. Stellen Sie sich selber vor:

Excuse me, I don't think we've met. My name is Meier.

The Right Word At The Right Time

"**How do you do?**" is a greeting not a question,
So don't tell your friends about your indigestion.

* * *

A visitor from the planet Mars landed in Bonn in front of the Kanzleramt. "**Excuse me, I'm from Mars.** Please take me to your leader." He was taken to the German Chancellor Helmut Kohl and introduced to the ministers of his cabinet. "**I'm pleased to meet you, gentlemen.** I've a message for your leader", said the man from Mars.
"**The pleasure is ours**," replied Helmut Kohl. "And please tell your company how much my wife and I enjoy your chocolate bars."

* * *

Bob: **Hello! I haven't met you during the last six months. What have you been doing?**
René: Six months. Cheating on the taxes.

* * *

On a bus, an absent-minded professor looked at the lady next to him and exclaimed: "**Hello**, Lydia Preston. **How are you? I haven't seen you in years. How you've changed!** You used to weigh 75 kilos and now you are nothing but skin and bones. Why Lydia, you've changed your hairstyle, too. You used to have grey hair and now you are blond....."
"I beg your pardon," said the lady, "but I'm not Lydia Preston."
"Fancy that," replied the professor, "You've changed your name as well."

* * *

Two elderly ladies met at a banquet after an absence of three weeks. Said the first, "Good gracious, Elizabeth, **I haven't seen you for years**. You certainly look a lot older."
"You look much older too, Dorothy, dear. I wouldn't have recognized you except for the dress and hat."

4. Einleitungen für Toasts und Trinksprüche

Sie sind auf einer englischen Party, und keiner spricht mit Ihnen – was tun? Versuchen Sie es mit der klassischen Methode. Nehmen Sie ein Glas und prosten Sie Ihren Nachbarn zu.

Good health!
Cheers!

Sollte dies nicht zu einer gepflegten Konversation über das Wetter führen, befolgen Sie bitte die Vorschläge im Kapitel *Starting and Ending Conversations, S. 13.*

Ein geselliges Zusammensein kann für Sie zum gesellschaftlichen Erfolg werden, wenn Sie hitzigen Diskussionen oder einer sich mühsam dahinschleppenden Konversation mit einem Trinkspruch eine unverhoffte Wende geben. Merke: Einen Toast kann man – mit Ausnahme der Dreieinigkeit – auf fast alles ausbringen.

Here's to *the lovely bride.*
I want to wish the best for…
I'd like to make a toast to *our new chairman.*
I rise to toast *an absent friend.*
I'd like to propose a toast to *the merger of our firms.*
Let's raise our glasses to *the future of our country.*

The Right Word At The Right Time

The newly-wed husband got up and raised his glass: "**Here's to** the lovely creature that has become my wife. Her voice is like a warm breeze in May. Her bright sunshine has dispelled the dark clouds of my depression. Her eyes are like..." Here his father-in-law interrupted him: "Is this a toast or the weather forecast?"

* * *

We had been waiting for ages for the waiter. "Gentlemen," said my father, raising an empty glass, "**I rise to toast** absent friends, among whom I include the waiter of this table."

* * *

"**Here is to** the beautiful bride. No matter how old you are, you don't look it."

* * *

The wedding party was drawing to its close. The father of the newly-wed husband got up: "**I raise my glass to** my beautiful daughter-in-law. May she give us lots of pretty grand-children". The bride, who had drunk a few glasses too many, staggered to her feet and stammered: "And I would like to thank my parents-in-law for giving me such a good perky copulator."

* * *

Bob: **Let's raise our glasses to** our host's excellent health. **May he live to** be one hundred years old and twenty days.
René: Thank you very much. But why the twenty days?
Bob: I certainly don't want you to die suddenly.

* * *

McNab and McTab, who were always arguing and fighting with each other, were finally approached by their vicar who took them to a pub, ordered two whiskies and said to them, "**Now raise your glasses** and make up."
They took their glasses, raised stiffly and McNab said: "**Here's wishing for you what you're wishing for me.**"
"Are you commencing aigain?" shouted McTab.

Test
The Right Word At The Right Time

1. Choose the most appropriate response.

"Four Tested Opening Lines" (Playboy, 1969)

1. I'm glad you don't recognize me. I'd rather have you love me for myself.
2. I don't dance. But I'd love to hold you while you do.
3. ______________. I'm Mr Right.
4. If national security were at stake, would you spend the night with a man whose name you don't even know?

a) I must say. *b) Congratulations on meeting me.*

c) I don't believe we've met. *d) I quite fancy you.*

2. Fit in an appropriate function or phrase.

After a fire in a well-known Greek restaurant the director got hundreds of letters with more or less the same wording: "______________. It's the first time the food's been hot in your place."

3. Match up the sentences in the two columns.

René says:	Robert replies:
1. That was a great meal.	a) Thanks, it took a lot of effort.
2. Full marks.	b) Thanks, I didn't expect to do so well.
3. My goodness, I've passed with top marks.	c) Thank you very much for your present.
4. I'd like to compliment you on your work.	d) Well, congratulations.
5. Best wishes on your birthday.	e) Yes, it couldn't have been better.

4. Give the most appropriate function for the German in the brackets.

(Viel Glück) on your sub-way ride.

Would You Do Me A Favour?

Die Kunst des Bittens

Sollten Sie zu den Glücklichen zählen, denen man auch im Ausland alle Wünsche von den Augen abliest, dürfen Sie dieses Kapitel getrost überspringen. Gehören Sie aber zu jenen, denen man keine roten Teppiche ausrollt, gelangen Sie nur durch die Beachtung sprachlicher Spielregeln an das Ziel Ihrer Wünsche. Die folgenden Sprachstrategien wollen Sie diesem Ziel ein gutes Stück näher bringen.

Die Kunst des Bittens

1. Was Sie vermeiden sollten

Selbst Führungskräften ist bei der Anleitung ihrer Mitarbeiter von allzu "spontaner" Willensäußerung abzuraten:

I want *more cooperation.*
What I want is *better team work.*
I want you to work *a little harder.*

Meiden Sie **Imperative,** sie verhallen ungehört.	Wer mit **I wish** beginnt, zweifelt an der Erfüllung seines Wunsches.
Rest *in peace.* ***Let's*** *be reasonable.* ***Don't let us*** *quarrel.* ***Please,*** *keep moving.* ***Kindly fill*** *in the coupon.*	***I wish I hadn't*** *eaten so much.* ***I wish you would*** *save some money.* ***I do wish you could*** *love me.*
Nackten Imperativen schicke man ein **please** voraus.	Zu erwartende Reaktion: **Take it easy.**

Wenden Sie sich nur in Notfällen an mehrere "Wohltäter" zugleich. Es könnte sich keiner angesprochen fühlen:

Who is willing to *put me up for a couple of days?*
Who would *lend me his car for the weekend?*
Who would be kind enough to *help me out with some change?*
Could anyone *drive me to Victoria Station?*

Would You Do Me A Favour?

The other evening I invited René and his girlfriend for dinner. My five-year-old daughter was allowed to serve the drinks. She stood there watching them and finally she said, "**I want to** see your trick?"
"What trick?", asked René.
"Well, Dad always says you drink like a fish."

* * *

Italian general to his troops at the end of World War I:
"When the enemy gets within one hundred metres of us, **I want you all to** start retreating. Being a little lame I'm leaving now."

* * *

"**I don't want you to** use those bad words again."
"But Mother, Shakespeare uses them."
"Well, don't play with him again."

* * *

A sign in an English holiday camp:
"Welcome to sunny Brightbeach – and **please, do not** leave wet raincoats, umbrellas and rubber boots in the bedrooms."

* * *

My car is so old that pupils always scrawl on it: "**Rust** in peace."

* * *

Attendant in chamber of horrors:
"**Please keep** your husband moving, sir. We're stock-taking."

* * *

The poor man was praying to God for wealth:
"My Lord! **Please let me** win the pools."
And God thundered: "Meet me halfways. **Kindly fill in** the coupon."

* * *

Teacher: **I wish you would** pay a little attention.
Student: But I'm paying as little as I can.

Die Kunst des Bittens

2. Wünsche ankündigen

Erfolgreiche Bittsteller machen sich zuerst vorsichtig mit einem kleinen Räuspern (Er...) und einer Entschuldigung bemerkbar. In einem zweiten Schritt künden Sie Ihre Bitte um eine Gefälligkeit an.

Er, excuse me, ... ***Er, I say...***	***Er, I beg your pardon,...*** ***Er, Mr Smith,...***

Could you do me a favour?
Would you do me a favour?
I wonder if you could help me.

Mit diesem sprachlichen Vorspiel haben Sie den Partner auf Ihre nun folgenden Wünsche hinreichend eingestimmt.

3. Wünsche äußern

Es ist höflich, auch kleinere Wünsche und Bitten an Freunde und Bekannte als Frage zu formulieren.

Is it alright if I *put the drinks on your bill?*
You haven't got *five pence for me,* ***have you?***
Have you got *a 5 pence piece for the telephone for me?*
May I trouble you for *some more coffee?*
Can / Could / May I have *some more meat, please?*

Would You Do Me A Favour?

The holiday charter flight had its usual number of children. One little boy in particular was getting on everybody's nerves by running up and down shouting and upsetting drinks. An elderly gentleman finally grabbed him by the arm and said: "Sonny, **would you do me a favour**? Please go and play outside."

* * *

Wife: It says here that marriage makes people look alike and I know that I'm beginning to talk like you.
Husband: **Do me a favour** and don't talk like a fool.

* * *

Son: Mum, I don't want to go to school. The teachers hate me and so do the kids. **Is it all right if** I stay in bed today?
Mother: No son, I'm afraid, you have got to go. After all, you are the headmaster.

* * *

A woman rushed into a shop and said, "**Can I have** a mousetrap, please? And will you be quick. I've got a bus to catch."
"Sorry, madam," said the assistant, "we don't have them that big."

* * *

A famous surgeon took a knife
To operate on Ronny's wife.
Said Ron: "**May I have** a word with you?
Could you sew her mouth up, too?"

* * *

Policeman: You were doing 50 m.p.h.
Motorist: **Please, could you** put 90 m.p.h. on the summons? Then I can show it to the man I'm trying to sell this car to.

Die Kunst des Bittens

Wir werden etwas höflicher, sind aber immer noch sicher, daß unserer Bitte entsprochen wird:

You couldn't *put us up for a couple of days,* ***could you?***
Do you think you could *show me the sights of the town?*
Would you mind *lending me your raincoat?*

Es wird Ihnen keineswegs als orientalische Unterwürfigkeit ausgelegt, wenn Sie eine Bitte wie folgt einleiten:

I wonder if I might *borrow your lawn-mower.*
I wonder if I might *take a day off.*
I wonder if I could trouble you *for a moment.*
I wonder if you would mind *doing a few extra hours.*
I wonder if you could possibly *post this letter for me.*
If I could have *a word with you,* ***I would be very grateful.***
Would you be so kind as to *help me with this letter?*
Could I possibly *leave a bit earlier today?*

Im Umgang mit Vorgesetzten ist Wortreichtum Gebot der Stunde:

I hope you don't mind me asking, but I wonder if you could possibly *advance me some money.*
I'm sorry to trouble you, but I wonder if it might be at all possible for you to *raise my salary.*

Would You Do Me A Favour?

He: Can you see alright? She: Yes.
He: You're not sitting in a draught? She: No.
He: Comfortable seat? She: Yes, fine.
He: **Would you mind** changing places?

* * *

A man travelling in the sleeping compartment of a train was woken up by someone tapping from below. "Are you awake?" asked a female voice. "Yes, what is it?" – "It's terribly cold down here. **I wonder if you would mind** letting me have another blanket?" – "I've got a better idea," answered the man. "Let's pretend we are married." – "That's a lovely idea!" giggled the woman. – "Okay then," said the man, "and now get your own damn blanket!"

* * *

A farmer's letter to the Ministry of Agriculture:
"Dear Sir,
I'm sorry to trouble you again, but this morning I found another of my prize chickens stiff and cold upon the ground. **Would you be kind enough to** tell me what the matter is?"
A few days later he got this reply:
"Dear Sir,
This chicken is dead, too."

* * *

The mother of one of the servants came storming into Lord Gray's office, demanding to see him. "**What is it you want?**" asked the lord. "It's about my daughter, Anne – she works for you," said the angry woman. "You've got her pregnant!"
"Well," replied the lord. "If she really is pregnant then I'll give her twenty thousand pounds a year. Does that seem fair?"
"You're very generous," agreed the woman. "But what if she isn't pregnant? **Would you be so kind as to** give her another chance?"

Die Kunst des Bittens

4. Wünsche erfragen

Und so lesen Sie Ihren Mitmenschen Wünsche von den Augen ab:

What can I do for you?	***What would you like?***
What will you have, *tea or coffee?*	***Do you want a*** *beer?*
How would you like *your tea?*	***Would you like to*** *stay?*
Would you like me *to go?*	***Shall I*** *turn off the TV?*

What is it you want? (unhöflich)

5. Wünsche erfüllen

Der Brite ist wortkarg, wenn er Bitten erhört:

Is it alright if...?	***Sure. / Certainly.***
May I use your phone?	***Go ahead!***
Can I have this photo?	***Here you are!***
I could do with a drink.	***Well, yes. Help yourself!***
Could I stay for the night?	***Yes, of course.***
I wonder if I could use...	***Yes, why not?***
Could I go now, please?	***By all means!***
Do you mind if I smoke?	***That's perfectly alright.***
Do you think you could help me with my homework?	***With pleasure.*** / ***I'd be glad to.***
Do you mind me smoking?	***Of course I don't.***
Mind if I shut the window?	***Not at all.***

Would You Do Me A Favour?

Two astronauts knocked at the gate of Heaven. St. Peter opened it, looked at them and said: "**Would you please** wait a moment, I'll check your files and see whether you may come in."
"Actually, we don't want to come in yet," said one of them.
"Really?" said St. Peter, "**Then what can I do for you?**"
"**We're so sorry to trouble you, but we were wondering if we might possibly** have our satellite back?"

* * *

English waiter: **How would you like** your coffee, sir?
American tourist: Just like my women – strong and sweet.
English waiter: Quite, sir. Er, black or white?

* * *

"Psst!" said the slimy looking man to the bridegroom.
"Do you have any photos of your wife in the nude?"
"Of course not!" growled the groom.
"**Do you want to** buy some?"

* * *

It was raining. A gentleman was leaving the ambassador's dinner party when he saw an elegant young lady waiting for the rain to stop.
"**Excuse me**," he said politely, "**may I** take you home in my car?"
"**Sure**," was the reply, "Where do you live?"

* * *

Little Anne was taken by her father to a séance at the home of a friend. The well-known medium asked the girl if there was anyone she would like to talk to. "**Do you think I could** talk to my old grandmother?" Anne wanted to know. – "**Certainly** my dear," said the medium, went into trance and began to talk in a strange voice: "This is your old grandmother speaking from Heaven. **Would you like to** ask me something, my child?"
"**Yes, of course**. Why are you speaking from Heaven when you're not even dead yet?"

Die Kunst des Bittens

6. Wünsche ablehnen

Bei der Ablehnung wäre es unhöflich, mit Worten zu sparen. Man wähle die Form: "Entschuldigung + Ausrede".

I'm sorry, I can't really. *There's a law against it.*
I'm afraid I couldn't. *You see, this car belongs to my boss.*
I'd like to say yes, *but I'm afraid I have a train to catch.*
Sorry. Not just now. I'm afraid I *really haven't got the time.*
I'm awfully sorry, *but you see I'm broke myself.*

* * *

"All the little boys and girls who want to go to Heaven, ***please stand up****", said the Sunday school teacher. All rose but Johnny. "Why Johnny,* ***wouldn't you like to*** *go to Heaven with the others?" – "****I'm afraid, I wouldn't*** *– not yet."*

* * *

Firefly (Groucho Marx) and Mrs Teasdale:
"Oh, er, I suppose you'll think me a sentimental old fool, but, er, ***would you be so kind as to*** *give me a lock of your hair?" – "A lock of my hair?* ***You can't really****... Why, I had no idea..." – "I'm letting you off easy. I was going to ask for the whole wig."*

Would You Do Me A Favour?

"**Er, I say, old man**," said Ronny to the host of the party, "there's this pretty young girl whom I'm getting on really well with, if you know what I mean. And **I wondered if I might possibly** use your spare bedroom for a while."
"**Sorry. Not just now**," replied the host, "**I'm afraid** your wife wouldn't like it."
"Oh, don't bother about her. I'm sure she won't miss me."
"I know that she won't miss you," said the host, "**but she's** just using that spare bedroom herself."

* * *

Clerk: **Er, I beg your pardon, sir. Could I possibly** take a day off to help my wife with the spring cleaning?
Boss: **I'm afraid you can't**. You see, just at the moment...
Clerk: Thank you, sir. I knew I could rely on you.

* * *

Father: **Could I** have a parrot for my son, please?
Pet-shop owner: **I'm awfully sorry, sir, but we** don't swop.

* * *

Young pupil: **Can I have** a cigarette, Miss?
Young teacher: **Good heavens! No, certainly not.** Do you want to get me into trouble?
Young pupil: Well, alright then, Miss. But I'd rather have a cigarette.

* * *

"**Waiter, could I have** some burned chips, cold beans, and sausages coated in cold fat?"
"**I'm sorry, sir, we couldn't possibly do that.**"
"Why not? You did yesterday."

Test
Would You Do Me A Favour?

1. Choose the most appropriate response.

A well-known psychiatrist got the following postcard from one of his patients: "I'm having a wonderful holiday on the Bahamas: ____________ here to tell me what is wrong."

a) Kindly be | *b) I wonder if you would mind being*
c) I wish you would come | *d) Do you think you could be*

2. Fit in an appropriate function or phrase.

Patient: Doctor, ____________ but could you possibly give me something for my flat feet?

Doctor: Let me see your feet. Good heavens! Well, hmmm..... what about a bicycle pump?

3. Match up the sentences in the two columns.

René says:	Robert replies:
1. Would you be so kind as to help me with this suitcase?	a) I'm afraid I couldn't. There's a law against it.
2. Do you think you could come round on Saturday evening?	b) I wish I could but I hate the places.
3. Could you pay me the money without a receipt?	c) If I can.
4. Who would go to the hospital with me?	d) Sorry, I won't be able to.
5. Would you do me a favour?	e) Of course. No trouble at all.

4. Give the most appropriate function for the German in the brackets.

Boss: Miss Smith, *(würden Sie bitte so freundlich sein und)* stop singing while you're working.

Miss Smith: Oh, I'm not working.

I'm A Bit Worried

Ich mache mir Sorgen

Gerade im Ausland können Problemchen zu Problemen werden. Doch auch hier gilt: "Geteiltes Leid ist halbes Leid." Teilen Sie Ihre Sorgen, indem Sie sich mitteilen. So don't worry! Auch im Ausland werden Sie mit den passenden Sprechfunktionen bei Ihren Mitmenschen immer Gehör finden.

Ich mache mir Sorgen

1. Politiker in Krisensituationen

Der Engländer ist bekannt für kühle Besonnenheit. Dies gilt in besonderem Maße für Träger von Verantwortung in Industrie und Politik. Sie verleihen in Katastrophen und Krisen ihrer Besorgnis mit etwa diesen Worten Ausdruck:

There's no reason to be alarmed, but...
We have some cause for concern.
We're / I'm concerned about...
I'm afraid we've got a bit of a problem here.

Der politische Gegner wird dasselbe Ereignis so kommentieren:

It's disturbing that...
We are alarmed that...
There's every reason for anxiety.
The worst possible thing has happened.

2. Das Ansprechen von Problemen des Alltags

Der gewöhnliche Bürger spricht seine Alltagssorgen so an:

I'm a bit worried about...
It's worrying that...
I'm / a bit / rather / very worried about...
The trouble is...

I'm A Bit Worried

Mrs Margaret Thatcher woke her husband up and said: "Denis, **there's no reason to be alarmed, but** there must be a burglar downstairs. Ring 999 while I make sure that he doesn't escape."
"Just a minute, Maggie," said her shivering husband. "Who shall I call, police or ambulance?"

* * *

A debate in the House of Commons. A Labour MP attacked the government: "**We are alarmed that** old people in this country are living from hand to mouth. What is the government going to do about this?"
Mrs Thatcher replied: "**We, too, are concerned about** the situation of our old citizens, but **there is no reason to be alarmed. It's just that** they have to do without the luxuries of life, such as television, housing, clothing, food..."

* * *

Young girl: Doctor, **I'm afraid I've got a bit of a problem**. This new diet you put me on makes me feel so sexy. I got carried away last night and bit off my boyfriend's left ear.
Doctor: **Don't worry!** It only has about forty or fifty calories.

* * *

Young girl: Doctor, **I'm very worried about** having a baby.
Doctor: You have no reason to be alarmed. I gave you the pill, didn't I?
Young girl: Yes, I know, but **the trouble is** it keeps falling out.

* * *

René: **I'm a bit concerned about** that letter I got the other day. It said: 'If you don't stop making love to my wife I'm going to kill you.'
Bob: So what's the problem? Leave her alone!
René: **The trouble is** it wasn't signed.

Ich mache mir Sorgen

3. In auswegloser Lage

Selten werden Engländer ihre Hilflosigkeit so direkt eingestehen:

I don't know what to do.
I don't know what I shall do.
I don't know which way to turn.
I'm at the end of my tether.
I'm at my wits' end.

4. In Situationen existentieller Bedrohung

Doch in Situationen höchster existentieller Bedrohung gibt auch der sonst so beherrschte Engländer seine Zurückhaltung auf:

I'm scared.
I'm frightened.
I'm worried/frightened stiff.
I'm scared to death.

Mit kräftigen Bildern der Umgangssprache weist er darauf hin, daß Sorgen nicht nur die Seele, sondern auch den Körper belasten:

I've got cold feet.	Ich habe kalte Füße.
I've got the jitters.	Ich hab' 'nen Mordsbammel.
I'm sweating cobs.	Ich schwitze Blut und Wasser.
He's got butterflies.	Er macht sich vor Angst in die Hose.

I'm A Bit Worried

Mr. Smith: Doctor, doctor! Please come quickly. My wife has terrible pains. It's the appendix. Be quick. **I really don't know what to do**.

Doctor: Let's calm down. You know as well as I do I took out your wife's appendix ten years ago. Have you ever heard of anybody having a second appendix?

Mr. Smith: Haven't you heard of anybody having a second wife?

* * *

Patient: **Doctor, I really don't know what to do**. If this swelling in my leg gets worse I won't be able to get my trousers on.

Doctor: Don't worry! I'll give you a prescription.

Patient: What is it for?

Doctor: A kilt.

* * *

Patient: Doctor, **I'm worried stiff about** this operation. What are my chances of surviving?

Doctor: Excellent. Nine out of ten patients die under this operation and the last nine I've operated on have died.

* * *

After his usual pub crawl, Tom knocked at the door of his church minister. "Reverend," he said, "**I'm frightened to death about** the doctrine of predestination."
"Look," said the minister, "why not come back in the morning, when you are in a better condition to discuss theological matters?"
"No," said Tom. "When I'm sober, I don't care a damn about predestination."

* * *

First burglar: The police! Quick! Let's jump out of the window!

Second burglar: I can't. We are on the thirteenth floor and **I've got the jitters**.

First burglar: Jump! This is not the moment to be superstitious.

Ich mache mir Sorgen

5. Erste Hilfe für Besorgte

Menschen mit Kummer und Sorgen suchen ein offenes Ohr und Gesprächsbereitschaft. Mit zwei *Sprachzügen* helfen Sie Ihrem Partner, sein Herz auszuschütten:

Mit dem ersten *Sprachzug* geben Sie ein Zeichen, daß Sie von den Sorgen des anderen Notiz nehmen.

Are you sure that you are okay?
You don't quite look your usual self.
You don't seem to be very happy.
You look as if you've seen a ghost.

Oft bedarf es des zweiten *Sprachzugs*, um Ihrem Gegenüber die Zunge zu lösen:

What's the problem today?
What's wrong?
What's the matter with you?
What's bothering you?
What's the trouble?
Is anything wrong?

Das folgende Kapitel ***Don't Worry, Be Happy*** zeigt Ihnen, wie Sie nach geduldigem Zuhören Trost spenden und wieder Mut machen können.

I'm A Bit Worried

The absent-minded Scottish professor, who was obviously not the best driver, took a continental colleague driving in the mountains. "**You don't seem to be very happy**," he said to his guest after a while. "**Is there anything wrong?**"
"Not really," was the reply. "It's only that **I'm frightened stiff** every time you go round one of those sharp curves."
"Then why don't you do as I do?" the professor asked. "Just close your eyes."

* * *

Little Bobby stared a long time at the stork in the zoo. "**You don't seem to be very happy**," said his mother. "**What's bothering you?"**
With tears in his eyes the boy turned to his mother and sighed, "He never even recognized me."

* * *

Bob: **What's wrong with you? You look as if you've seen a ghost**.
René: I was at the doctor's and he told me to take a pill every day for the rest of my life.
Bob: **Where's the problem?** That's not so bad.
René: No? He only gave me five.

* * *

Doctor: **Now, what's the matter with you**?
Patient: Doc, I've just swallowed rat poison. What shall I do?
Doctor: Repeat after me, 'Our Father which are in Heaven...'

* * *

Psychiatrist: Well, **what is bothering you**?
Patient: Doctor, **I'm very much concerned about my wife**. She thinks I'm a kangaroo.
Psychiatrist: Tell your wife I would like to have a word with her. And now hop off... and mind your tail when you shut the door.

Test
I'm A Bit Worried

1. Choose the most appropriate response.

Patient: Doctor, doctor. ____________ about something. Everybody thinks I'm a liar.

Doctor: Hmmmm! I find this very hard to believe.

a) I'm alarmed *b) I'm a bit worried*
c) I have some cause for concern *d) I'm sweating cobs*

2. Match up the sentences in the two columns.

René says:	Robert replies:
1. You look as if you've seen a ghost.	a) Now, just take it easy a minute
2. What's bothering you?	b) Okay, let's discuss it.
3. I'm at my wits' end.	c) That's a bit of an exaggeration surely.
4. We've got a bit of a problem here.	d) Yes, I've had quite a bad shock.
5. The worst possible thing has happened.	e) Well, I've got a bit of a pain in the stomach.

3. Give the most appropriate function for the German in the brackets.

Two very seasick Irishmen were returning to Ireland by boat.

Tom: Mick, *(ich kann nicht mehr)*. Tell the captain to stop the ship for a few minutes until I get a rest... or I'll have to get out and walk.

4. What would you say if...

you were on a sailing boat and you suddenly noticed there was a hole in it with water coming in?

a) The trouble is... *b) We have some cause for concern.*
c) I've got cold feet. *d) I've got butterflies.*

Don't Worry! Be Happy!

Das rechte Wort bei Pech und Pannen

Nicht immer ist Schweigen Gold. Stellen Sie sich vor, Ihnen widerfährt ein Mißgeschick. Würden Sie nicht ein paar Worte der Anteilnahme erwarten?

Zur Pflege mitmenschlicher Beziehungen benötigen Sie die Redemittel der Anteilnahme und der Aufmunterung. Wem die rechten Worte fehlen, gilt als Unmensch.

Das rechte Wort bei Pech und Pannen

1. Erste Reaktionen bei Pleiten, Pech und Pannen

Wenn Ihren Mitmenschen etwas schiefgeht, dürfen Sie nicht sprachlos bleiben. Bis Ihnen die passenden Worte einfallen, gewinnen Sie Zeit mit dem beruhigenden, **verneinten Imperativ**.

Don't worry!	*Don't be afraid.*
Don't you worry!	*Don't be depressed.*
Don't let it worry you.	*Don't take it so hard.*
Don't lose your head.	*Don't get excited.*
Don't be sad.	*Don't give up hope.*
Don't be alarmed.	*Don't look on the black side.*

Gute Freunde und Familienmitglieder darf man sogar auffordern, im Unglücksfall eine positive geistige oder körperliche Haltung einzunehmen.

Bear up!	*Chin up!*
Keep calm!	*Take it easy!*
Keep a stiff upper lip!	*Just relax!*
Try to forget it.	*Come on!*

Let's cross our fingers.

Mit energischeren Formulierungen holt man den Freund bei Panik und hysterischen Anfällen auf den Boden der Realität zurück.

Keep your hair on!	*Pull yourself together!*
Put it out of your mind!	*Don't lose heart!*

Don't Worry! Be Happy!

René: I'd like to see the doctor immediately.
Receptionist: He won't be able to see you before June 12th.
René: No sooner than that? I could be dead by then.
Receptionist: **Don't let it worry you**, you can always cancel your appointment.

* * *

We were on a very stormy sea voyage and my wife was very seasick. The captain came to our table and said to her:
"**Don't worry**, you'll live." – "Don't say that," whispered my wife, "it's only the thought of dying that keeps me alive."

* * *

A lady belonging to the world's oldest profession went to the doctor feeling quite poorly. After a thorough examination the doctor said: "**Chin up**! We'll soon have you back on your back."

* * *

The village undertaker was visiting his gravely ill friend in hospital. "**Bear up**! You can always count on me. I'll be the last one to put you down. So **don't give up hope**."

* * *

The other day I bought a very expensive new wool suit. At home I saw the label saying '100% cotton'. I took it back to the shop and complained.
"**Don't be alarmed**," said the shop assistant, "it's merely a trick to fool the moths."

* * *

Peter: I've got degrees in psychology, politics and economics – and still I can't get a job.
Bob: **Don't look on the black side**, at least you understand why you can't.

Das rechte Wort bei Pech und Pannen

2. Anteilnahme, Trost und Aufmunterung aussprechen

Die folgenden **Aussagesätze** wirken persönlicher als die stereotypen bejahten oder verneinten Imperative. Sie dienen als Einleitungen und Aufhänger für weitere trostreiche Worte, die der jeweiligen Situation anzupassen sind.

There's nothing to worry about.
There's no need to worry. *I'll handle it for you.*
I wouldn't worry.
You'll get over it.
There are much worse things.
Things could be worse.
There's nothing to panic about.

3. Wie man Pechvögeln Hoffnung machen kann

I hope *you aren't hurt.*
I hope it *will turn out alright.*
I really hope…
I really do hope…
I assure you it will be alright.
We mustn't give up hope.
Let's hope…
Let's hope for the best.
We can only hope that…
Where there's life there's hope.
It'll turn out alright / okay.

Don't Worry! Be Happy!

Psychiatrist: **I wouldn't worry too much about** your son making mud pies.
Worried mother: Well, I do worry – and so does his wife.

* * *

Kohn and Greenstein, who were partners, were lunching one day. Suddenly Kohn shouted: "My God, I left the safe open."
"**There's no need to worry**," replied Greenstein, "we're both here, aren't we?"

* * *

Hein and Otto, two East-Friesians, were flying for the first time when there was a cry "Fire! The plane has caught fire!"
Otto became hysterical but Hein comforted him by saying:
"**There's nothing to panic about**. The fire isn't in our half of the plane."

* * *

Doctor: Good afternoon, Mrs Jones. I've just received the results of your tests. **There is nothing to be worried about**. I've got good news for you, Mrs Jones.
Patient: Doctor – I'm Miss Davis!
Doctor: Oh, hmm... in that case, Miss Davis, I've got bad news for you.

* * *

The captain of a Boeing 747 had forgotten to switch off the intercom and so the passengers could overhear the captain say in the cockpit: "I'll have a cup of coffee and then screw that new stewardess."
The stewardess at the other end of the plane turned red and ran down the cabin to warn the crew that the intercom was on. But in her haste she tripped and fell. An elderly lady helped her get up and comforted her:
"I hope you haven't hurt yourself. **Keep calm**! Let him finish his coffee first."

Test
Don't Worry! Be Happy!

1. Choose the most appropriate response.

René: ________________. Everything will be alright.
Bob: I wish I could believe you. But at the moment my wife drives me to drink.
René: You're lucky. I have to walk.

a) Pull yourself together! *b) Don't get excited.*
c) Don't be sad! *d) There are much worse things.*

2. Fit in an appropriate function or phrase.

Psychiatrist: And what can I do for you?
Husband: You've got to help me. My wife talks to flowers.
Psychiatrist: ______________. She'll get over it. A lot of ladies do it.
Husband: To flowers on the wallpaper?

3. Match up the sentences in the two columns.

René says:
1. I hope her husband doesn't hear us.
2. Oh dear me, whatever will I do?
3. My God! All that money thrown away.
4. I thought she would always love me.
5. I hope you aren't hurt.

Robert replies:
a) Don't be alarmed. It's only a small operation.
b) Keep your hair on. It's only a car.
c) Well, it was a bit of a shock.
d) You'll get over it.
e) Yes, let's cross our fingers.

4. Give the most appropriate function for the German in the brackets.

Soldier: And what happens if the parachute fails to open?
Sergeant: *(Darüber müssen Sie sich keine Sorgen machen.)* Bring it back and you'll get another.

Tell Them What You Think

Wie Sie Ihre Meinung sagen

Bekanntschaften folgen einer gewissen Eigengesetzlichkeit. Zuerst werden Lebensläufe ausgetauscht, danach spricht man von Beruf und Hobby, schließlich über Urlaub und Krankheiten. Aber was dann, wenn der Datenaustausch abgeschlossen ist? Sie können die Konversation auf eine höhere Ebene heben, wenn Sie Ihren Gesprächspartner nach seiner Meinung zu bereits behandelten Themen fragen und mit Ihrer Meinung auch nicht hinter dem Berg zurückhalten.

Wie Sie Ihre Meinung sagen

1. Meinung erfragen – Meinung sagen

In einem ersten Schritt sollen Sie das Rüstzeug für den Standardaustausch von Meinungen erwerben.

Eine Meinung erfragen:
Do you think that…? *What do you think of…?* *What is your opinion about…?* *Do you want to say that…?* *Do you mean that…?* *You mean…?* *What do you consider…?* *Do you believe that / in…?*

Und seine Meinung sagen:
Well, I reckon that… *I think…* *If you ask my opinion…* *In my opinion…* *If you ask me…* *It seems to me that…* *I'd say (that)…*

Tell Them What You Think

It was on their wedding evening and they were about to go to bed when he asked suddenly: “Darling, **what do you think of** the Middle East position?” A little embarrassed she replied: “How should I know, Darling? Are we going to try it?”

* * *

Psychiatrist: **How long have you believed** in reincarnation?
Patient: Ever since I was a frog.

* * *

Grandmother was accompanying two little girls around the zoo. While they were looking at the stork, she explained to them that it was this bird that brought the little babies. The girls looked at each other and one whispered to the other: “**Do you think** we ought to tell Grandma the truth?”

* * *

René: **Do you think** your son will forget everything that he learned at school?
Bob: I hope so. He can’t make a living by kissing girls.

* * *

The wife wanted to do some shopping so she asked her husband for some money. “Money, money, money!” he shouted. “Every day of the week you want more money. **If you ask me**, I think you need brains more than you need money.”
“Maybe”, his wife agreed, “but I asked you for what **I thought** you had the most of.”

* * *

Two committees in the American government have the same function but different names. The one in the *House of Representatives* is called *Committee on Foreign Affairs;* the one in the *Senate Committee on Foreign Relations.* When asked by an astonished foreign correspondent, why there were two names, one of the elderly senators gave this answer: “**Well, I reckon** we senators are too old to have affairs.”

Tell Them What You Think

Teacher: **What do you consider** the greatest achievement of the Romans?
Pupil: Speaking Latin.

* * *

Irish Pat was once convicted of murder and just after the sentence had been passed he confessed that he had actually been in prison when the crime was committed.
"Why on earth didn't you tell the court that?" his lawyer asked.
"**I thought** it might prejudice the jury against me."

* * *

After an uneventful 7 years of friendship Anne said to René, "René, **it seems to me** it's high time we were getting married."
"Don't be a fool, woman," replied René, "who would marry either of us at this stage of our lives?"

* * *

The philosophical goldfish suddenly stopped swimming round in his bowl and turned to his companion: "I say, can you see any purpose in our swimming round and round? I can't. **It's my belief that** God doesn't exist." – "Don't be silly," replied the other goldfish. "**Who do you suppose** changes our water?"

* * *

Beckenbauer to Mayer-Vorfelder:
"I've finally selected a football team and **I'm pretty sure** they will win the next world cup. It's Brazil."

* * *

Judge: I find the defendant not guilty.
Defendant: **Do you mean** that I can keep the money?

* * *

Bob: How's your friend, the hypochondriac? **Does he still think** he's sick?
Anne: Oh, no. **Now he's convinced** he's dead.

Tell Them What You Think

Anne: You remind me of the sea.
René: **You mean** I'm wild, restless and romantic?
Anne: No. You make me feel sick.

* * *

A tourist was picking flowers on Farmer Doorbar's farm when he suddenly noticed an enormous bull. He shouted to the farmer who was working nearby: "Is the bull safe?"
"Well, **I'd say** he's a lot safer than you are at the moment."

* * *

Graffiti and humorous quotations:

If God really made everything, **I'd say**
he has a quality control problem.

* * *

I believe that sex is a beautiful thing between two people.
Between *five*, it's fantastic.
Woody Allen, The Nightclub Years, 1972

* * *

I didn't believe in reincarnation the last time either.

* * *

Written on the wall of a public lavatory among many other graffiti:
One would think from all this wit
That Shakespeare himself came here to shit.
Someone had written beneath it:
If you ask me, well, it may be true
For Shakespeare had to do it, too.

* * *

For some people work is a pain in the neck.
However **I have** a much lower **opinion of it**.

Wie Sie Ihre Meinung sagen

Je stärker Sie von sich überzeugt sind, desto mehr werden Sie von der zweiten oder letzten Gruppe sprachlicher Aufhänger Gebrauch machen.

Vorsichtige Meinungsäußerung

It seems to me that...
It looks as if...
It appears to me...
Well, I would tend to think that...

Subjektive Überzeugung

I presume...
In my view...
As I/we see it...

Starke Überzeugung

I'm quite sure that...
It's my belief that...
I'm convinced that...
I'm dead certain that...

Tell Them What You Think

When Margaret Thatcher was visiting the British troops in Germany she was asked to attend a big dinner party.
"**Well, it seems to me that** your soldiers prefer wine, women and song to doing their job," she remarked to one of the officers.
"No, they don't care for music," was the reply.

* * *

McNab's nephew came to him with a problem.
"I've a choice of two women," he told him, "a beautiful but poor girl of 19, who I love dearly, and a rich but ugly old widow."
"**In my view** you should marry the girl you love," said McNab.
"I'll follow your advice," said the nephew.
"In that case," said McNab, "could you give me the widow's address?"

* * *

René: **Why do you think** so many people take an instant dislike to me?
Bob: Hm . . . well, **if you ask me, I'd say** they want to save time.

* * *

Bob: **Do you believe** in ghosts?
René: I don't, but I know they are there and **I presume** they don't believe in me either.

* * *

A journalist asked Churchill **why he thought** he had lived so long.
"**Well, I'm convinced that** it's the whisky and the cigars."
"Nothing else?" the journalist wanted to know.
"Just one more thing – cancelling my voyage on the Titanic."

* * *

It's my firm belief that I'm not a dirty old man – I'm a sexy senior citizen.

Dr. René Bosewitz

Wie Sie Ihre Meinung sagen

2. Meinung mit persönlicher Note

Die ganz persönliche Note geben Sie subjektiven Meinungsbeiträgen mit folgenden idiomatischen Floskeln:

Personally, I think…
Frankly,…
If you ask me…
As far as I'm concerned, I think…
Let me put it this way…
In my eyes…

3. Sprachzüge für Meinungsstarke

Für charakterstarke Menschen mit unerschütterlichen Überzeugungen empfehlen wir diese sprachlichen Schachzüge:

Der Meinung sein, daß…	**Nicht der Meinung sein, daß…**
I'll say this about…	***I don't want to say anything about…***
I believe in…	***I don't believe in…***
I'm in favour of…	***Personally, I'm against…***
I support…	***I oppose, / reject…***
I approve of…	***I disapprove of…***
I'm campaigning for…	***I'm campaigning against…***

Tell Them What You Think

And Jesus said to them: "**Now, frankly, who do you think** I am?"
And after a short time of hard thinking and consulting, Peter spoke up: "**We are convinced that** you are the eschatological manifestation of the ground of our existence, the kerygma of which we find the ultimate meaning in our interpersonal relationships."
And Jesus said, "WHAT?"

* * *

"**I personally don't believe** in supersonic overseas transports."
"Because you are conservative?"
"No, because I lisp."

* * *

Bob: I've read so much about smoking and drinking. **As far as I'm concerned**, I've decided to give it up.
René: Smoking or drinking?
Bob: Nonsense! Reading.

* * *

René: **What do you mean**, I'm a failure?
Anne: **Well, let me put it this way** – ours is the only house in the street that hasn't been burgled.

* * *

Angry teacher: **Frankly**, you must be the laziest fellow in the world.
Pupil, with a smile: **Personally**, I don't think so. That would be too much of a coincidence.

* * *

I'm campaigning against early retirement for married men. It **appears to me that** it means twice as much husband on half as much money.

Alice Schwartzer (attrib.)

Test
Tell Them What You Think

1. Choose the most appropriate response.

Young man: ________________ you could be happy with a man like me?

Young girl: Of course! As long as he wasn't too much like you.

a) As far as I'm concerned *b) Do you think*
c) Personally, I think *d) In my view*

2. Match up the sentences in the two columns.

René says:	Robert replies:
1. If you ask my opinion they'll never get married.	a) Yes, you're quite right.
2. I presume that you're Mr Hohrein?	b) It doesn't look like it.
3. It's my belief that history will repeat itself.	c) Yes, it certainly looks that way.
4. I'm campaigning for more rights for foreigners.	d) Well, you're entitled to your opinion.
5. Let me put it this way. You're lazy.	e) Well, good luck.

3. Give the most appropriate function for the German in the brackets.

She: Arthur?
He: Yes, love.
She: *(Ich glaube)* I'd like to be cremated.
He: Okay love – get your coat on.

4. What would you say if...

you won the pools?

a) Frankly, it's great. *b) I'm campaigning for it.*
c) I'm in favour of it. *d) It's my belief that it's great.*

How To Agree With People

Einer Meinung sein

"*Einverstanden*" und "*Abgemacht*" gehören mit zu den schönsten Worten, mit denen man Gespräche und Verhandlungen abschließen kann. Ein Händeschütteln und ein Trinkspruch* auf den Vertrag ist oft der Beginn einer fruchtbaren Partnerschaft.

* Passende Trinksprüche siehe S. 48

Einer Meinung sein

1. Mit jemandem einer Meinung sein

Agreed.
I agree.
Quite true. Quite right.
I think so, too.
I don't mind.
I accept that.
I think we are in agreement.

2. Sich einer Argumentation beugen

I see your point.
You've got a point there.
That's a good point.
I can go along with that.
That seems okay / reasonable.

3. Zustimmung aus taktischen Gründen

Mit diesen *speech functions* stimmen Sie Ihrem Partner zu. Mit einem angehängten ***but*** oder ***however*** können Sie aber auch dem Kontrahenten mit einem Gegenargument in die Parade fahren:

You've got a point there, but...
I can see that. On the other hand, however,...
I would tend to agree with that, if only...
That seems acceptable, however,...

How To Agree With People

A preacher to his Scottish congregation:
"**I accept that** you put buttons in the collection plate, **but** please bring your own buttons and don't pull them off the church cushions."

* * *

A hen-pecked husband got back from the pub and announced: "I'm fed up with married life. I'm going to join the Foreign Legion."
"**I don't mind**," said the wife, "but don't you dare come back in here treading sand all over the place."

* * *

Patient: Are you sure I'll get well? I heard about a doctor who was treating a patient for TB and he died of malaria.
Doctor: Yes, **I would tend to agree that** some doctors don't know what they're doing. **But** when I treat a man for TB he dies of TB and nothing else.

* * *

Graffito in China:
In our country rape is impossible!
Written beneath:
I see your point! Women with skirts up can
run faster than men with trousers down.

* * *

"I've a complaint to make," said a woman to the purser on a holiday cruise. "A sailor peeped into my cabin last night when I was undressing. I think that's absolutely scandalous."
"**I think so too,**" said the purser, "**but** what do you expect for second class – the captain?"

* * *

"Don't you find a baby brightens up the house wonderfully?"
"**Quite true** – we've the light on most of the night."

Einer Meinung sein

Mit folgenden Ausdrücken der bewundernden Zustimmung dürfen Sie sogar die Reden Ihres Chefs begleiten oder unterbrechen. Er wird Sie dann auch bei künftigen Entscheidungen immer zu Rate ziehen.

4. Ausrufe der Zustimmung

Absolutely!
Definitely!
Precisely!

5. Rückhaltlose Zustimmung

Längere Denkpausen Ihres Gesprächspartners füllen Sie mit etwas ausführlicherer Zustimmung. So schaffen Sie sich Freunde.

That goes without saying.
That's just what I was thinking.
I'm of your opinion.
I quite/totally/entirely agree.
You are quite right.

Fahren Sie nach diesen Ausdrücken mit einem ***but*** oder ***however*** fort, nehmen Sie Ihre Zustimmung wieder teilweise zurück und leiten ein Gegenargument ein.

How To Agree With People

Graffito:
"The meek shall inherit the earth," says Jesus.
Written beneath:
Definitely! But not its mineral rights.

* * *

Married man: In your sermon this morning, vicar, you said it was wrong for people to profit from other people's mistakes. **Do you really agree with that**?

Vicar: **Absolutely**!

Married man: In that case, will you consider refunding the ten pounds I paid you for marrying me to my wife seven years ago?

* * *

A tourist visiting Brighton stopped at a hotel for an early evening drink. In the bar he got to know a very attractive girl. After a few drinks he took her over to the reception desk and booked a double room for the night, signing in as Mr and Mrs Doorbar. The next morning after breakfast he was presented with a bill for £1000.
"What's all this?", he exclaimed. "I've only been here one night, haven't I?"
"**You're quite right**, Mr Doorbar," said the clerk, "but your wife has been here for five weeks."

* * *

Graffito:
ENGLISHMEN MAKE THE BEST LOVERS!
You've got a point there, but the
Japanese make them smaller and cheaper.

* * *

JESUS IS THE ANSWER!
I quite agree, but what was the question?

Test
How To Agree With People

1. Choose the most appropriate response.

Bob: My wife said I was to ask for a rise, sir.
Boss: __________ I'll ask my wife if I can give you one.

a) You've got a point there. *b) I quite agree.*
c) Precisely. *d) That goes without saying.*

2. Fit in an appropriate function or phrase.

They lay close together.
"I'm probably the first man you've made love to," he said. She studied him reflectively.
"________________. Your face certainly looks familiar."

3. Match up the sentences in the two columns.

René says:	Robert replies:
1. We should concentrate more on getting fit.	a) That's just what I was thinking. I'm overweight.
2. Perhaps we ought to rewrite this book.	b) Agreed. I need a bit of relaxation.
3. So we all want to play billiards tonight.	c) Definitely not.
4. We can't accept what they're offering us.	d) I tend to agree because of the mistakes.
5. It's time to leave this country. What do you think?	e) I can certainly go along with that.

4. Give the most appropriate function for the German in the brackets.

Once there was a young vicar who had just got married. He and his bride were ready to taste the fruits of love. But before the eager bride could climb into bed, he suggested they should kneel and pray for strength and guidance.
"*(Einverstanden)*", she said, "but you just pray for strength and I'll do the rest."

Disagreeing With People

Anderer Meinung sein

Was dem Araber das Feilschen, ist dem Engländer sein Kompromiß. ***Compromising*** ist ja bekanntlich eine Volkstugend der Briten. Doch fällt Ihnen der Kompromiß nicht einfach in den Schoß. Weder beim Araber noch beim Engländer erzielen Sie ein Ergebnis ohne Argument und Gegenargument. In diesem Kapitel lernen Sie, auf fünf verschiedenen Registern des Widerspruchs zu spielen.

Anderer Meinung sein

1. Understatement

In besseren englischen Kreisen erfreut sich das ***understatement*** noch großer Beliebtheit. Wo der Kontinentaleuropäer sagt: "Ich bin entschieden anderer Meinung", begnügt sich der Brite mit einem interessierten ***Oh!*** oder einem freundlichen ***How extraordinary!***

Oh!
Is that so?
Would you believe it!
Really?
How interesting?
Are you sure?

2. Vorsichtiger Widerspruch

Wie das ***understatement*** ist auch der vorsichtige Widerspruch ernster zu nehmen, als er klingt.

I'm not so sure.
Do you really think so?
I think there's more to it than that.
I'm not totally convinced.
I don't altogether/quite agree with you.
Hm..., I'm not so sure I agree.
I'm afraid it's not as easy/simple as that.
I'm afraid I don't share your view.
I'm afraid I can't quite agree with you.
I see it a little differently.
We'll have to agree to differ.

Disagreeing With People

An extremely fat lady was sunbathing on the beach, when she was approached by a lifeguard.
"Excuse me, madam", he said, "but hadn't you better move?"
"**Really**," she replied, "why on earth should I?"
"The tide is waiting for you to let it in."

* * *

Lady Wilberforce rang for the hotel manager, who came up immediately.
"It's disgraceful!" she complained. "In the room opposite there is a man doing press-ups and sit-ups – completely naked!"
The manager looked out of the window. Then he said:
"Well, **I'm not so sure**. **It's true** there is a man **although** I can only see his head."
"**Is that so**?" said the lady angrily. "Well, you just stand on this chair."

* * *

The two Irish engineers were having difficulties measuring the flagpole in front of the Limerick Town Hall. A German tourist suggested that they lay it on the ground and then measure it correctly.
"**I'm afraid it's not as easy as that,**," said one of them, " We're trying to measure its height, not its length."

* * *

Carmen:	Wow, your new boyfriend is a very good-looking man.
Rosalita:	Well, **I can't agree with you there**. If you think he's good-looking you should have seen the 'Juan' that got away.

Anderer Meinung sein

3. Die "JA – ABER"-Taktik

Eine beliebte Taktik von Politikern und Verhandlungsstrategen ist es, dem Gegner scheinbar zuzustimmen, um ihm das Wort zu entreißen und dann mit einem ABER zu kontern.

I see what you mean, but/although…
You may be right. Even so…
You seem to have a point there. All the same…
I don't disagree altogether. Still…
I believe you. Nevertheless…

4. Entschiedener Widerspruch

I can't agree.
I don't think so.
I disagree entirely.
I just don't agree.
I can't believe it.
I doubt it.
I very much doubt that.
You are completely mistaken.
To be quite frank, I can't go along with you.
To put it bluntly, it's quite wrong to say…
It's alright for you to talk, but…

5. Emotionale Ausrufe des Widerspruchs

Definitely not!
Rubbish!
Give over!
Nonsense!
Ridiculous!
Come off it!
You must be joking!

Disagreeing With People

Tailor: Your suit will be ready in six months, sir.
Client: Six months! **I really can't accept that**. It took only six days to make the whole world.
Tailor: Yes, indeed – but have you noticed the shape it is in?

* * *

In the middle of the election campaign a Labour MP and an MP from the Conservative party meet in a pub. "Well, what have you told your voters today?" asked the conservative.
"I've told them that the rich should give to the poor," said the Labour man.
"**I doubt that** they will follow your advice."
"Of course they will! I'm half way there already. The poor have agreed."

* * *

Pete, a third-rate magician, came bursting into his agent's office.
"Bob, I've got an idea for a new trick."
"That's what you always say, Pete. What is it this time?"
"I saw a woman in half", Pete said triumphantly.
"**Come off it**! It's been done a million times before."
"What", cried Pete, "lengthways?"

* * *

Let me tell you my first disappointment as a financial adviser. I tried to explain to an eighty-year-old millionaire how I would double his investment in four years.
"**You must be joking**," he shouted at me. "At my age one doesn't even buy green bananas."

* * *

Optician: You need glasses!
Annette: **I doubt it**. What makes you think so?
Optician: I knew as soon as you walked in through the window.

Disagreeing With People

Anne: **Nonsense**! I can't really believe that you'll kill yourself if I refuse to go to bed with you. **That's ridiculous**.
René: It has been my usual procedure until now. So don't provoke me.

* * *

A young couple were planning to go on a boat trip in Ireland. "Let's take my mother with us. She would love it", suggested the wife. Her husband was not pleased. "**No**! **Definitely not**! She will ruin the whole trip. You know what she is like."
They had a row for several days, finally the husband gave in and rang up his mother-in-law in order to invite her. "Too late," was the reply, "I've already prayed for rain!"

* * *

At a hospital in Ireland:

Mary: I want to see an out-turn.
Nurse: **I don't think so**. You mean an intern.
Mary: Oh, well. I want a contamination anyway.
Nurse: **It's completely wrong to say** 'contamination'. You want an examination, don't you?
Mary: Alright, in any case I want to go to the fraternity ward.
Nurse: **I very much doubt that**. It's the maternity ward you want.
Mary: What the hell! Fraternity, maternity, out-turn, intern, contamination, examination. All I know is that I haven't demonstrated for three months and I think I'm stagnant.

* * *

Bob: Hair cut please. What does that cost?
Hairdresser: Hm . . . for you DM 40.
Bob: **Come off it**! That's robbery. How much is a shave?
Hairdresser: DM 20.
Bob: Could you shave my head please.

Test
Disagreeing With People

1. Choose the most appropriate response:

René: I think you should leave your job and do something else.
Bob: Oh dear, ________________. You've got a good job. To tell the truth I don't think I could do anything else.
René: Bob, you've got to be flexible.
Bob: I reckon I'm getting too old to be flexible.

a) we'll have to agree to differ. *c) I see what you mean.*
b) I see it a little differently. *d) it's alright for you to talk.*

2. Fit in an appropriate function or phrase.

An election poster read: The Labour Party is the answer!
Underneath somebody had written:
"I'm afraid ________________. If they're the answer it must have been a pretty stupid question."

3. Match up the sentences in the two columns.

René says:	Robert replies:
1. I think Jenny is arrogant.	a. I believe you, but you should take it easy before it's too late.
2. We should send all the foreigners home.	b. To be frank, I don't agree with you.
3. I saw you in the cinema with another woman.	c. You are completely mistaken.
4. We just can't come to a decision.	d. No, we'll have to agree to differ.
5. I'm totally overworked.	e. Well, I see it a little differently.

4. Give the most appropriate function for the German in the brackets.

Chemist: These contraceptives are more expensive because they are guaranteed by the makers.
Customer: I'm *(nicht hundertprozentig überzeugt)*. What if they break?
Chemist: Then the guarantee runs out!

Sit Back And Smile

The head of one of the big Chicago Mafia families was accused of murder, blackmail, rape and few other crimes. The jury was out for nine hours. When they came back into the courtroom the judge asked them if they had come to a decision. The foreman rose and said timidly, "Yes, Your Honour, we decided not to become involved."

* * *

An elderly lady entered a pet shop and said to the shop assistant, "You sold me this canary bird yesterday and I've found out that it's a little lame."
"What do you want," replied the shop assistant, "a singer or a dancer?"

* * *

The Moscow paper, Pravda, had Ivan Jacobowsky's name in the obituary column. Ivan wrote to the editor: "I'm not dead, but you have my name in the obituary column. I want a retraction."
This is what the editor wrote back:
"Dear Ivan,
Pravda doesn't make mistakes. If it says you are dead, you are dead. But here is what we can do for you. Tomorrow your name will be put in the birth notices."

* * *

The religious instructor asked his pupils, "Have you done your good deed today?"
"Yes," said Johnny eagerly. "Me and five other boys carried an old gentleman across a busy street."
The teacher smiled, "That was a fine thing to do, but did it take six of you to help an old man across the street?"
"Yes. He didn't want to go."

Granting Permission

Erlauben und Verbieten

Sie sind ein Erfolgsmensch? Sie leben nach dem Motto "Im Anfang war die Tat" und "Wer viel fragt, bekommt viele Antworten"? Herzlichen Glückwunsch! Ignorieren Sie den ***Erlaubnisteil*** dieses Kapitels. Er wäre der weiteren Verfolgung Ihrer Karriere nur abträglich.

Sie, liebe Leser, die nach dem Motto "Mit dem Hute in der Hand, kommt man durch das ganze Land" leben müssen, lernen, wie Sie darum bitten, etwas tun zu dürfen – und wie man es Ihnen abschlägt.

Erlauben und Verbieten

1. Standesgemäß um Erlaubnis bitten

Vier häufig verwendete Einleitungen für **Bitten um Erlaubnis**:

May I…
Can I…
Could I…
Please, let me…
Please, allow me…

Hier sind weitere nützliche "Sprachzüge", angeordnet nach dem zu erwartenden Widerstand und der Tiefe Ihres Knickses bzw. Dieners:

Asking for permission:

I'd like to *leave a bit earlier today.*
Alright if I *try on the blouse in the window?*
Are we allowed/permitted to *fish?*
Anyone mind if I *open the window?*

Do you mind if I…?
Is it alright if I *pull the fish out now?*
Would it be alright if I…?
Would you mind if I *try?*

I wonder if I could possibly *wear lipstick?*
I hope you don't mind, but would it be possible if…?
I'm sorry to bother you, but could you *lend me your…?*
Permit me to…

Granting Permission

Bob: I'm afraid this meat doesn't agree with me. **Alright if I** give it to the dog?
René: No, Bob, that is the dog.

* * *

A 60 year old but sexually still very active Hollywood star to the young pop group she was sponsoring:
"The one who guesses my age **may** sleep with me tonight." There was a long and embarrassed silence. Finally the brightest of the young musicians had an idea: "Thirty-five, madam."
"Close enough," said the lady with her sweetest smile.

* * *

Ronny: Mummy! Mummy! **Can I** go for a swim in the sea?
Mother: No dear. **I'm afraid you can't**.
Ronny; But Daddy's gone in.
Mother: He's insured.

* * *

Judge: Not guilty of bigamy. **You may** go home.
Accused: Thank you, Your Honour. Which one?

* * *

Patient: **You don't mind if I** kiss you, Nurse.
Nurse: **You certainly may not**.
Patient: Come on, don't be prudish. **Please, let me** kiss you.
Nurse: No, sir – and **I'm not even permitted to** be in bed with you.

* * *

The pastor, astonished to see an unusually large Easter congregation, thought for a moment and announced:
"Dear brothers in God, I'm afraid I shall not see many of you again until next Easter, so **permit me** to take the opportunity to wish you a merry Christmas and a very happy New Year."

Erlauben und Verbieten

2. Erlaubnis erteilen und verweigern

Freundliche Engländer werden Ihrer Bitte entsprechen und Ihnen dies wie folgt zu erkennen geben:

Yes, of course.	***Yes, go ahead.***
You are welcome.	***Yes, I suppose.***

Oh well, alright.

Und so werden in Großbritannien Bittsteller abgewiesen, wobei es zum guten Ton gehört, eine Ablehnung zu begründen.

If I were you, I wouldn't…
Wouldn't it be better if you didn't…?
I'm afraid you can't…
I'd rather you didn't, if you don't mind.
I'm sorry, but it's not possible.

Vermeiden Sie kategorische oder unbegründete Ablehnungen wie:

No.	***You may not.***
I'm sorry.	***You are not allowed to…***

Hat man Sie abschlägig beschieden, geben Sie bitte nicht gleich auf. **So leiten Sie Ihre Argumente ein:**

Well, you see…
The reason is…
Let me explain…
…that's why I'd like to…

Granting Permission

"Mum, I'm fifteen today and **I wonder if I could possibly** put on eye-shadow, lipstick and perfume and wear high-heeled shoes?"
"No, Ronny, **I'd rather you didn't**."

* * *

Prince Charles was on a fishing trip with a native fisherman in the Caribbean when he suddenly felt a nibble on his line.

Prince: **Is it alright if I** pull him out now?

Native: **If I were you I wouldn't**, Your Majesty... Oh, ...not yet. I'd rather you didn't, Your Highness. ...For Christ's sake, **stop pulling**, Your Lordship. ...My God, now you've lost him, you bloody foreigner.

* * *

A lady went into a shop and asked, "**May I** try on that nice blue blouse in the window?" – "Well," replied the shop assistant doubtfully. "**I'm afraid you cannot**, there are too many people outside. Wouldn't it be better to use the fitting-room?"

* * *

After a particularly boring morning at school little Ronny asked: "**Alright if** we go home now, Miss?" – "**I'm sorry, but it's not possible**," replied the teacher. "The bell hasn't gone yet."
"But Miss!" insisted the boy, "only yesterday you told us not to leave everything to the last minute."

* * *

A very attractive girl was about to enter the church in a topless dress when the vicar ran towards her. "**I'm very sorry, madam**," said the vicar, "**but I cannot possibly allow you to** go into my church like that."
"But I've a divine right," protested the girl.
"Yes," agreed the vicar, "and a divine left, too, but still **I cannot allow you** into my church like that."

Granting Permission

"Please, bartender, **could I possibly** have two cherries in my cocktail? My doctor told me I should eat more fruit."

* * *

Ronny walked up to the ticket office of a cinema, bought a ticket and went inside. A moment later he came out and bought another one and went in again. This happened several times until the ticket lady finally said:
"**May I** ask, sir, why you are buying so many tickets?"
"Sure, there's a crazy woman in there. Every time I give her my ticket, she tears it up."

* * *

Russian leader Gorbachev was being shown round the workshops of one of Britain's largest chemical companies. He was astonished to see the British workers filing in up to one hour late.
"That's nothing," replied his guide. "They break off for tea at ten, take an extra thirty minutes for lunch and then go home up to half an hour before knocking-off time."
"In Russia **they would not be allowed to** do that," said Gorbachev. "They start at seven and work full ten hours."
"You couldn't get them to do that here," sneered the guide, "they're all bloody communists."

* * *

Ronny: You've gone too far. **You allow me to make** love to you only twice a week.
Anne: What are you complaining about. I've cut off some of our tenants completely.

Test
Granting Permission

1. Choose the most appropriate response.

"Doctor, doctor! I keep thinking I'm a dog."
"Well, have a seat and calm down."
"Oh no, ________________ sit on the furniture."

a) Alright if I...?
b) I'm not allowed to...
c) Would you mind if I didn't...?
d) Please, let me...

2. Fit in an appropriate function or phrase.

Bob: I'm sorry I'm late for school, sir.
Teacher: Can't you get up a bit earlier?
Bob: ________________ explain, sir. I was having a dream about football.
Teacher: Why did that make you late?
Bob: They played extra time.

3. Give the most appropriate function for the German in the brackets.

The best-known drinker in an Irish village staggering homeward, met the Parish priest. This gentleman asked, *(hätten Sie was dagegen, wenn ich)* look in your pocket? I think there's a bottle in it." "*(Ja selbstverständlich, machen Sie nur.)* It's holy water", said the drunkard. The priest took the bottle out, smelled it and shouted that it contained whisky. "Well, praise be to God," cried the drunk, "A miracle!"

4. What would you say if...

you found a stranger putting your coat on after the theatre performance?

a) Would you mind discussing something?
b) Would it be alright if we talked?
c) We must talk.
d) I'm sorry to bother you but could I have a word with you.

Relax And Rejoice

Mrs Dean to her husband:
"Take off my coat and my shoes." Mr Dean does so. "Now my blouse... my skirt, my bra... now the rest of my underwear... and Neal, if I ever catch you wearing them again, I'll leave you."

* * *

Three old men trembling with age used to spend the afternoons sitting together watching cars and people passing by. One day a reporter wanted to find out the secret of their long lives.
"What is your hobby?", he asked the first.
"My hobby is chess. Sometimes I play a game for three weeks."
"And what's your age?"
"I'm eighty-seven."
The reporter turned to the second man and asked him the same questions.
"I play the violin and I listen to classical music. Sometimes I stay up all night without sleep." Asked for his age, he replied: "I'm ninety-three."
The last one was even more tottering and shaking than his two friends and when asked about his hobbies he replied: "Well, I drink a bottle of whisky a day, I smoke twelve cigars and I go to the brothel twice a week."
"Remarkable!" exclaimed the reporter, "and how old are you?"
"Thirty-four."

* * *

A man and his wife were on holiday at the seaside. One morning, they were walking along the promenade when a seagull flew overhead and left its calling card on the wife's new dress. Her husband found this highly amusing, but his wife cried angrily, "Don't stand there laughing! Get some paper!"
"What's the good?" said the husband. "That bird will be miles away by now!"

Giving Instructions

Anleiten, Gebieten, Verbieten

Verhaltensänderungen bei Mitmenschen erreicht man unter anderem durch Ge- und Verbote. *Thou shalt not...*, heißt es in der Bibel. Da dieser Gebots- und Verbotsaufhänger Göttern, Propheten und Pfarrern vorbehalten ist, benötigen Polizei und ähnliche Institutionen andere sprachliche Mittel, um uns auf den rechten Weg zu bringen.

Anleiten, Gebieten, Verbieten

1. Anweisungen, Ge- und Verbote von existentieller Wichtigkeit

Allein diese Seite rechtfertigt Ihre Ausgaben für dieses Buch. Auch wer der Schule sonst eher feindlich gesinnt ist, sollte die Redemittel zumindest passiv beherrschen. Die aktive Beherrschung wird all jenen empfohlen, die schon immer nach Rettungsmedaillen und Verdienstkreuzen strebten.

Mind your *head!*	***Mind*** *where you are treading.*
Watch your *step!*	***Watch out for...!***
Beware of *the dog!*	***Dangerous*** *crossing.*
Don't *cross the lines.*	***Keep out!*** *Explosives!*
Look out!	***Watch it!***
Handle with care!	***Don't*** *lean out of the window!*

2. Anweisungen und Gebote praktischer Natur:

Vor allem jene Menschen, denen bei ihren Anstrengungen, ein Schuhschränkchen nach Gebrauchsanweisung zusammenzusetzen, regelmäßig Schrauben übrigbleiben oder fehlen, werden Ihren Anleitungen besonders dankbar Folge leisten.

The first thing you have to do is...
First of all you...
After you have done that you...
The next thing you do is...
Then you...
And be careful not to...
Don't forget to...
Make sure that...
And remember to...

Giving Instructions

Xerox your life – if you lose it, it's nice to have a copy.

* * *

Road safety notice outside a school:
Drive carefully. **Don't kill** a child.
Wait for a teacher.

* * *

Don't play ping-pong with an open mouth.

* * *

Doctor: How did you have this accident?
Patient: The traffic sign said: **STOP, LOOK, LISTEN**. And while I did the train hit me.

* * *

Doctor: **Say** 'aaaaaah.'
Young lady: That's a change! Most young men want me to say 'yes'.

* * *

Rules For Managers From Murphy's Laws:

1. **Never be** first.
2. **Never be** last.
3. **Never volunteer** for anything.

A. Bloch

* * *

Written on the electric handdryer in one of the Bundestag toilets:
Press this button for a fifty second speech from our chancellor.

* * *

Graffito:
In case of atomic attack:
First you put your hands over your ears.
Then you put your head between your legs.
And don't forget to kiss your ass goodbye.

3. Gebote und Verbote ethischer Natur

Kategorische Imperative zur Läuterung des Lebenswandels der Mitmenschen gehören zum Bordwerkzeug jedes Pädagogen:

Mind your language!
Watch what you say!
Be good!
Don't walk on the grass!
Don't sin/smoke/lie/fight!
Stop causing pollution!
Love your enemy!

Wer die Direktheit des Imperativs scheut, formuliert Appelle an das Gewissen seiner Partner mit Hilfe der modalen Hilfsverben:

Gebote: Modale Hilfsverben:

You/I must *be on time/do your homework.*
You/I should *always tell the truth.*
You/I ought to *pay our taxes.*

Andere Verben:

You/I've got to...
You are to/I am to...
You are/I'm supposed to...

Giving Instructions

Here are a few graffiti trying to mend the ways of the world:

This graffito was found on the door of Trinity Church in Chicago:
And the angel said unto the shepherds:
"**Shove off**. This is cattle country."

* * *

Prepare to meet God (evening dress optional).

* * *

Poster in a church: **Love** Thy Neighbour
Someone had added: – Regularly!!

* * *

On the door of the biology classroom: **Make** Love Not War.
Scribbled beneath: **See** teacher for details.

* * *

Young girl in a cinema: **Take** your hand **off** my knee!
No, not ***you, YOU!***

* * *

René: What are you doing there, Bob? **Don't you dare** pull faces at my bulldog.
Bob: I'm not to blame. He started it.

* * *

Anne and René at the airport:
She: **You should have** brought the piano.
He: Why?
She: Our tickets are on it.

* * *

"I've prepared the turkey," said René to his girlfriend. "I've plucked it and stuffed it. **All you've got to do** is kill it and cook it."

Giving Instructions

Mother: Ronny's teacher says **he ought to have** an encyclopedia.
Father: Nonsense. Let him walk to school like I did.

* * *

Susan was doing the shopping with her mother. A vicar approached, wearing ordinary clothes. "Good morning Vicar!" said her mother. "How do you know he's a vicar?" asked Susan – "**I should** know him," replied her mother, "he's the man that married me."
"In that case," cried Susan, "who's that man hanging around our house that I call 'Father'?"

* * *

Father Benedict rang up the police to ask that a dead donkey be removed from the gate of his churchyard. The officer who took the call thought he would be smart: "I thought it was the Church that took care of the dead," he said.
"You're right, son," said Father Benedict. "But first **we have to** get in touch with the relatives."

* * *

"If you want to work here, young man," said the managing director, "one thing **you must** learn is that we are very keen on cleanliness in this firm. Did you wipe your feet on the mat as you came in?"
"Yes, of course, sir," replied the applicant.
"And there is another thing **you must** learn," the director went on. "We are very keen on honesty: there is no mat."

* * *

Scotsman to St. Peter at the gate of Heaven: "You must be bored with your job showing people in, century after century."
St. Peter replied with a smile: "**You must remember**, here in Heaven things are different. A million years are but as one second and a million pounds are but as one penny."
– "Could you give me a penny, please?"
– "Of course – in a second."

Giving Instructions

The pretty girl was explaining her idea of the ideal husband to her boyfriend: "The man I marry **must be** musical; **he should be able to** tell jokes and to sing and he must stay at home in the evenings."
"What you need," said her boyfriend, "is a television set."

* * *

Doctor: Well now, is your cough better this morning?
Patient: **It should be**. I've been practising all night.

* * *

A missionary went to a remote part of the world to teach some natives. One of his less successful lectures went like this:
"All men are your brothers and **you must** love your brothers."
The natives raised their spears and shouted: "Owamba! Owamba!" – "But **you ought to** love your enemies as well." The natives raised their spears and shouted: "Owamba! Owamba!" The missionary went on: "If a man hits you, **you should** turn the other cheek." Again a raising of spears and a loud "Owamba! Owamba!"
"**Thou shalt not** kill," he went on. "Therefore **the Church expects you not to** fight." Once again, the natives raised their spears and shouted: "Owamba! Owamba!"
The missionary was very satisfied with the effect his speech had had on the whole tribe and stepping down from the platform he said to his guide: "I think my little speech went down well, don't you?" – "Well," said his guide, "I don't know... **Watch your step**! Don't tread in the owamba."

* * *

Groucho Marx didn't think much of stuntmen:
"An amateur thinks it is funny if you dress a man up as an old lady, put him in a wheelchair, and give the wheelchair a push that sends it spinning down a slope towards a stone wall. For a professional, **it's got to** be a real old lady."

Anleiten, Gebieten, Verbieten

Aus dem Gebot wird ein Verbot, wenn man die folgenden modalen Hilfsverben verneint:

You mustn't…
You can't…
You may not…
***You shouldn't** do that.*
***You ought not / oughtn't to** say a word.*
***You didn't ought to** be so distrustful.*

Andere Verben:
You are not to…
You are not supposed to…
***We will have no more** arguing / coming late.*

4. Sach- und andere Zwänge

Ge- und Verbote, die sich nicht mit Moral oder Ethik rechtfertigen lassen, nennt man Gebote der Stunde oder auch Sachzwänge:

***I've (got) to** help him.*
I am to…
I've got no choice…
I'm supposed to…
I'm obliged to…
I'm compelled to…
I'm forced to…
I need to…
It's necessary…
It's obligatory for me…
It's compulsory for me to…
You are requested to…

Giving Instructions

Ronny was very sick indeed and was rushed to the hospital. After a brief examination the doctor announced to his wife and the nurse that Ronny was dead. "I'm not", cried Ronny weakly from his bed.
"**We'll have no more arguing**!" hissed the nurse, "or do you think you know better than the doctor?"

* * *

After Ronny had been away from home for two years, his wife had a baby.

Bob: I'm sorry to bother you, Ronny, but could I ask you a question? Aren't you a bit suspicious about this situation?

Ronny: My dear Bob, **you didn't ought to be** so distrustful. After all, there are five years between me and my sister.

* * *

Ronny was late for work one morning. So the excuse he made to the boss was that the train was late. His boss got very angry:
"**We'll have no more** arriving late. The next time the train is late come on the earlier train."

* * *

Sven, an East-Friesian, was having dinner with some friends in Ribbeck when a heavy snow storm set in. "**You can't possibly** go home in this weather," insisted his host. "**You are forced to** spend the night with us." – "That's very kind of you," replied Sven, "I'll just go home and bring my pyjamas."

* * *

"In some countries," said the geography teacher, "**men are supposed to** have more than one wife. That's called polygamy. In others, you are allowed more than one husband. That's polyandry. In this country, **we are obliged to** have only one married partner. Can anyone tell me what that's called?" A shy little girl raised her finger and asked in a whisper: "Monotony, sir?"

Giving Instructions

Bobby: Dad, can you help me please? Teacher said that tomorrow **we are supposed to** know what *reincarnation* is.

Father: Well, have a look in the fridge. And tell her that I find it particularly good on fruit salad.

* * *

Graffito on the door of a gents' toilet:
Clients **are requested** to remain
seated throughout the performance.

* * *

We all know that familiar sign in toilets on trains:
'**People are requested not to** use the toilet while the train is standing at a station.' Somebody had scribbled underneath:
EXCEPT AT INVERNESS.

* * *

Young girl: Teacher says there are certain things **a girl shouldn't do** before twenty.

Father: And right she is. I'm not too keen on an audience either.

* * *

McGregor was short of money, so he rang up his friend McTavish and asked for a loan of 5 pounds.
"Sorry," said McTavish, "**you've got to** speak up, I can't hear a word you're saying."
"Can you lend me 5 pounds?" screamed McGregor into the phone.
"Look," said McTavish, "the line is terrible. **You must** try it some other time."
At this stage the operator chipped in and said, "There's nothing wrong with the line, I can hear the caller distinctly."
"In that case, **you ought to** give him the money," retorted McTavish angrily.

Test
Giving Instructions

1. Choose the most appropriate response.

Vicar: Now, ________________ before we can get forgiveness of sin?

Girl: Sin.

a) stop doing it *b) watch it*
c) be careful not to do it *d) what have we got to do*

2. Fit in an appropriate function or phrase.

Mark Thatcher was on the losing crew in a boat race. His mother was trying to console him. "Now ________," she ordered him. "It wasn't your fault. You rowed much faster than anyone else in your boat."

3. Match up the sentences in the two columns.

René says:	Robert replies:
1. You should always tell the truth.	a) Oops, I nearly cut it again.
2. Be careful not to lose the keys.	b) Yes, I almost forgot it.
3. Mind your finger!	c) Yes, I'm not as safe on my feet as I used to be.
4. I need to get my money from you.	d) When did I not?
5. Watch it!	e) When did I ever lose them?

4. What would you say if...

you caught somebody using the toilet on a train while it was standing in the station?

a) Mind where you are treading. *b) Stop causing pollution.*
c) You are requested not to do that. *d) Don't cross the lines.*

Just For Fun

Bob: Do you have a family tree?
René: Family tree? – My family doesn't even have flower-pots.

* * *

Modern art: If you can hang it on a wall it is a painting. If you can walk around it, it is a sculpture.

* * *

Neal to his best friend's wife: "You know, I'd like to make love to you, Linda, just to find out which one of you is better in bed, you or my wife."
"You don't have to go to the trouble," said Linda. "Why don't you ask my husband. He'll tell you."

* * *

"... and you should welcome each guest by name," the hotel manager said to the new porter.
"But how will I know their names?" asked the new porter.
"That's simple," explained the manager. "Look at the luggage. Normally they have their names written on their suitcases."
So the first couple to enter the hotel and be welcomed by the porter were greeted: "Welcome, Mr and Mrs Genuine Pigskin".

* * *

It was a wet and stormy day when Abe buried his wife Barbara. Just as the funeral party left the graveyard there was a flash of lightning and a loud clap of thunder. Abe looked up to the sky and sighed: "Well, she's arrived up there already."

* * *

Bob: Did you hear what happened when Glen sent his picture to the Lonely Hearts Club?
René: No, what?
Bob: They sent it back. They said they weren't that lonely.

Giving And Taking Advice

Rat geben, Rat annehmen und ablehnen

Das Streben deutscher Politiker, rückständigen Völkern mit wohlgemeinten Ratschlägen den Weg des Heils zu weisen, hat ihnen weltweit zu Anerkennung verholfen. Nur bei Angelsachsen stoßen sie noch auf Undank, was sich durch viele Zitate belegen ließe.

The only thing to do with good advice is to pass it on.
It is never of any use to oneself. — *Oscar Wilde*

Nothing that is worth knowing can be taught. — *G. B. Shaw*

Rat geben, Rat annehmen und ablehnen

1. Der vorsichtige Ratgeber

Wollen Sie nicht Zeuge sein, wie Ihr britischer Mitmensch in sein Verderben läuft, zögern Sie nicht, ihm – wenn nötig ungefragt – zu seinem besten zu raten, und nehmen Sie das so ganz undeutsche sprachliche Vorspiel mit in Kauf:

Tarnen Sie Ihren Rat als vorsichtige Frage:

Might it be an idea if you *learnt a foreign language?*
Do you think it might be a good idea to *learn our language?*
I was wondering if you have ever thought of *learning German?*
Have you ever thought of *trying a German lawn-mower?*
Why not *drive on the right as everybody else?*
Why don't you *hide behind a tree...?*
Wouldn't it be better if *you bought/* ***to*** *buy a German hamster?*
Wouldn't it be wiser if...?
Hadn't you better use/try *Uhu Alleskleber?*
May/Can I give you a piece of advice? *Make the best of it.*

* * *

Anne: *How on earth can I prevent rice from sticking together?*
René: ***Well, why don't you*** *boil each grain separately?*

Giving And Taking Advice

Teacher: I'm afraid, Mrs Smith, that your son has not been his old self for the last few weeks. He keeps saying he is a cat. **Have you ever thought of** having him seen to?
Mother: But I did, and the vet says he's in perfect health.

* * *

Son: Daddy, what is the best way to catch a rabbit?
Father: Well, **why don't you** hide behind a tree and imitate the noise of a carrot?

* * *

René: I hate paying my income-tax.
Bob: **Be** a good citizen. **Why don't you** pay with a smile?
René: I'd like to but they insist on money.

* * *

Driving instructor: **Wouldn't it be better** if you slowed down?
Young lady: But I'm allowed to drive 50 miles an hour in this area.
Driving instructor: Yes, but not on the pavement.

* * *

Mr. Sutter: So you want to marry my daughter. **Don't you think you'd better** see my wife first?
René: I have, sir, and I still want to marry your daughter.

* * *

"Now that you are married, **may I give you a piece of advice?** Have some insurance."
"But why? My wife isn't dangerous."

* * *

Is it safe to create a problem for which you haven't got the answer? **Wouldn't it be wiser to** create problems for which only you have the answer?

Rat geben, Rat annehmen und ablehnen

2. Der deutliche Ratgeber

Mit belehrbaren Briten werden Sie deutlicher, vor allem, wenn man Sie tatsächlich einmal um Rat fragt.

Well, if you ask me, I'd *forbid football matches altogether.*
If I were *Thatcher,* ***I'd*** *send all hooligans to prison.*
If I had to do it, I'd *create special work camps for them.*
It might be better to *ban football fans from the island.*
You could always *say it was for the good of the country.*
The best thing to do is *to create an anti-hooligan squad.*
I advise you to *call in one of our specialists from Germany.*
I recommend you to *follow the example of German clubs.*

* * *

Daughter: *Tell me, what do you think makes a marriage successful?*
Mother: ***I think you'd better*** *ask your father. After all, he made a more successful marriage than I did.*

* * *

When I had my first baby my father sent me a nice present. When I had my fourth baby he sent me a book about birth-control and a card saying: ***You'd better read than breed.***

* * *

The best way to *stay out of the army* ***is to*** *join the navy.*

Giving And Taking Advice

If you want to eat well in England, **you could always** eat three breakfasts.

* * *

René: Your wife hasn't spoken to anybody in the family for more than six months. **If you ask me I'd** divorce her.

Bob: **That's all very well, but** wives like that are hard to get.

* * *

Wife: It's taken me almost an hour to write this message to the milkman.

Husband: **If I were you, I'd** write it on the paper before I put it into the bottle.

* * *

The mathematics professor and his fiancée were out strolling in a park when she picked a daisy and looking sweetly at him began to pull off the petals, saying: "He loves me, he loves me not..."
"You are giving yourself a lot of unnecessary trouble," said the professor. "**If I were you I would** count up the petals, and if the total is an even number, the answer will be in the negative, if an uneven number, in the affirmative."

* * *

Pretty young nurse: Every time I take this young man's pulse it gets faster and faster. Should I give him a sedative or something?

Doctor: No. **The best thing to do is to** blindfold him.

* * *

Doctor: Your heart is very weak. **I advise you to** play golf for your health.

Patient: But I play golf already.

Doctor: Then **I recommend** that you stop it.

* * *

"Doctor, doctor, do you think I'll live after this operation?"
"Sure. But **I wouldn't advise** it."

Rat geben, Rat annehmen und ablehnen

3. Der Mahner und Warner

Es ist Schicksal wohlmeinender Ratgeber, daß ihre Bemühungen oft zu Unrecht als Besserwisserei und Einmischung ausgelegt werden. Gutgemeinte Mahnungen wollen deshalb zuerst im privaten Bereich erprobt sein, bevor man damit Vorgesetzte vor Fehlern bewahrt.

Gebrauchen Sie den freundlichen Imperativ:

Be sure to *eat enough vegetables.*
Remember to *take your medicine.*
I should warn you. Be careful!
Advice to public speakers: ***Stand up, speak up, shut up.***

Stellen Sie die mahnende Frage:

Is it reasonable to *smoke that much?*
Is it wise to *drive that fast?*
Isn't it a bit risky to *trust this company?*
Is it safe to *lend this client so much money?*
Aren't we taking too many risks *if we...?*

Sprichwörter geben Ihrem Rat etwas Absolutes:

Prevention is the mother of care.
It's the early bird that catches the worm.
Silence is the virtue of those who are not wise.
In a calm sea every man is a pilot.

Wo guter Rat auf steinigen Boden fällt, ist es ratsam, den Strategien des Kapitels "**Nobody Is Perfect**" zu folgen.

Giving And Taking Advice

Sign in a bar: "If you suddenly notice our colour TV – **don't** drive. It's black and white."

* * *

Father: Why were you kept in again after school, son?
Son: I didn't know where the Bermuda Triangle was.
Father: Well, in future **remember** where you put things.

* * *

Advice for managers from A. Bloch. Murphy's Laws (adapted):

1. **Always try to** look very important.
2. **Try to** be seen with important people.
3. **Keep** out of sight and out of the limelight.

* * *

A woman of eighty visited her doctor: "I'm going to be married next week, doctor, and I'm a bit nervous."
"Congratulations," said the doctor. "How old is the bridegroom?"
"Eighteen," said the woman.
"My goodness!" exclaimed the doctor. "**Be careful! I should warn you that** too much activity in bed could be fatal."
"Well," said the woman. "If he dies, he dies."

* * *

Young husband: **Is it reasonable to** spend my income the way you do it? Think of the future. If I were to die, where would you be?
Young wife: Well, I'd be here alright, the question is where would you be?

* * *

A tourist in Austria was scared to walk so near a dangerous gorge and he said to his guide: "**Isn't it a bit risky to** have no warning signs in places like this?"
"Well," said the guide, "we used to have warning signs up for years but nobody fell over, so we took them down again."

Rat geben, Rat annehmen und ablehnen

4. Wie man guten Rat ablehnt

Das britische Empire wurde gegründet, um dem lieben Gott die Verantwortung für die Völker dieser Erde abzunehmen. Darum betrachtet sich auch der Brite als geborener Ratgeber. Seinen Rat können Sie mit folgenden Strategien parieren:

Do you really think I should...?
Are you really suggesting that I should...?
That's all very well, but...
That's easier said than done, you see...
You don't seem to realize that...
You seem to forget that...
You'd better mind your own business.
Mind your own business.
Nonsense! / Rubbish! / Ridiculous!

5. Guter Rat für aussichtslose Lagen

Guten Rat für Unglückliche in aussichtslosen Lagen wie Regen und Nebel in London oder Schiffskatastrophen kann man nicht allgemein genug halten. Mit folgenden Ratschlägen liegen Sie nicht nur immer richtig, sie erlauben es Ihnen auch, sich elegant vom Ort des Unheils zurückzuziehen.

Make the best of it!
Keep your hair on!
Keep your end up!
Take care of yourself!
Just wait and see!
Don't take it too seriously!
Don't get all worked up!
Take / Look after yourself!
Do be careful!
Take it easy!
Let it all hang out!

Giving And Taking Advice

Bob: I've lost my dog.
René: **Why don't you** put an advertisement in the paper?
Bob: **Rubbish! You seem to forget that** my dog can't read.

* * *

Mother: **Why don't you** give your husband a divorce?
Daughter: **Are you really suggesting that I should** divorce him now that I have supported him for more than ten years?

* * *

Patient: **Do you really think** I should go on taking these pills? They could be habit-forming.
Doctor: **Nonsense!** I've been taking them myself for years.

* * *

René was due to appear in court. He met a friend the night before who gave him the following advice: "**If I were you I would** send the judge a fine leather wallet and his wife some flowers."
The next morning René met his lawyer and told him of the conversation. "**Nonsense! Your friend had better mind his own business. You don't seem to realize that** we've already got a very weak case and an action like that would go against us." When the case came up, René won, to everybody's astonishment. "I never thought we had a chance," admitted the lawyer. "Did you really send the judge those presents?" – "Yes, of course," came the reply, "but I put the other party's name on it."

* * *

A fellow was complaining he was always tired. "**Why don't you go** to the doctor?" suggested his friend. So the chap went to the doctor, who asked him how often he had sex. He replied: "Monday, Tuesday, Wednesday, Thursday and Friday." Advised the doctor: "Well, I think you'd better cut out Fridays." – "**That's easier said than done**," said the chap, "Friday is the only day I'm at home."

Test
Giving And Taking Advice

1. Choose the most appropriate response.

René: Now look _______________. What's the problem?
Robert: I'm in love with her, she loves me, we both enjoy the same things, she earns plenty of money, we're really happy together... My problem is, what shall I tell my wife?

a) wouldn't it be better if you relaxed? *b) is it wise to get so excited?*
c) don't get all worked up. *d) make the best of it.*

2. Fit in an appropriate function or phrase.

In a barber's shop. Robert is getting a shave and manicure. He asks the attractive manicurist, "I was wondering if you've thought of going out to dinner with me tonight."
"I can't," she answers. "I'm married."
"Tell your husband that you're working tonight."
"_______________," says the manicurist. "He's shaving you."

3. Give the most appropriate function for the German in the brackets.

A French woman dies. At the funeral her husband is calm. Not at all upset. Her former lover can hardly control his anguish. He throws himself onto the coffin crying and shouting. The husband goes over to him. "*(Sie sollten sich lieber beruhigen)*. I plan to marry again."

4. What would you say if...

somebody had just trapped his finger in the door?

a) That's easier said than done. *b) Remember to put a bandage on.*
c) Be sure to be careful! *d) Keep your end up!*

Nobody Is Perfect

Kritisieren und kritisiert werden

Criticism is the disapproval of people having faults different from ours.

In diesem Kapitel erwerben Sie die sprachlichen Glacéhandschuhe für den Umgang mit Vorgesetzten, Polizisten und Fahrkartenkontrolleuren, aber auch die härteren Bandagen für den täglichen Ärger, sei es mit Mitarbeitern, Bediensteten oder engeren Familienmitgliedern.

Kritisieren und kritisiert werden

1. Mit der Zunge des Diplomaten

Wo Rücksicht auf den Chef und Personen, die man noch braucht, ratsam scheint, vermeidet der gebildete Engländer direkte Kritik. Er macht zuerst einen "sprachlichen Kniefall" in Form der kurzen Entschuldigungen oder Einleitungen, denen er dann den Vorwurf folgen läßt. Ein Oberkellner würde so formulieren: ***"Will you forgive me for saying so, but I'm afraid you forgot to pay the champagne and caviare, sir."*** Er denkt natürlich: ***"The damned old fool is trying to get away without paying again."***

Sehr höflich:
Will you forgive me for saying so, but... ***I hope you don't mind me saying this, but...*** ***I'm afraid I've got something to tell you.*** ***I'm afraid I'm not quite sure how to put this.*** ***I don't like to mention this, but...***
Höflich, freundschaftlich:
I'm sorry to bring this up, but... ***Excuse me but...*** ***Look, I'm sorry to trouble you, but...*** ***I'm sorry to have to say this, but...*** ***I've got a bit of a problem here...***

Wenn der Mächtige sich diese Redewendungen genüßlich auf der Zunge zergehen läßt, werden sie allerdings zu Instrumenten der Demütigung des weniger zungenfertigen Untergebenen.

Nobody Is Perfect

A doctor's receptionist rang up McNab: "Mr McNab, **I'm afraid I've something to tell you**. Is it possible that you haven't paid your account for the private visit you had over a month ago? The doctor is very upset."
"Okay," said McNab. "Tell him to take two aspirins and if he's no better – call me again next week."

* * *

The elderly filmstar was lying naked on the roof of her expensive hotel, sunbathing. Suddenly the manager came up to her, coughed politely, then said: "**I hope you don't mind me saying this, but I'm afraid** this is hardly the right place for nudity." – "**I don't really see the point**", said the actress, "there is nobody around."
"That may be so", replied the manager, "but you are lying on the skylight of the dining room and it is lunch time."

* * *

A certain German politician still thinks this a good joke:
Party leader Honnecker was lying in bed with his mistress.

She: Darling, **please forgive me for bringing this up again, but why** don't we pull down that nasty Berlin wall?

He: (after a long pause with a smile of relief):
Oh, I see what you mean, darling. You want to be alone with me, don't you?

* * *

A British minister's heroic last words:

Minister: Please, Prime Minister, could I leave now? I'm just too tired to work this afternoon.

Thatcher: **I'm sorry to have to tell you this, but** work has not killed any member of my government yet.

Minister: **You may be right**, Prime Minister, but why should I run the risk of being the first?

2. Der indirekte Vorwurf in Frageform: Kritik an Nahestehenden

Eine **indirekte und immer noch taktvolle Art und Weise**, Kritik **an Gleichgestellten oder Untergebenen** zu üben, ist die (oft rhetorische) Frage. Die kluge Ehefrau mag denken: ***"You are a hopeless alcoholic."*** Sie wird aber sagen: ***"Did you really have to drink the whole bottle of whisky?"*** Diese Art der Frage ist ein beliebtes **Erziehungsmittel** im Munde von Eltern und Lehrern.

Don't you think it would have been better to...?
Was it really necessary to *do that?*
Did you have to *work so hard?*
Do you really think you ought to... / should...?
Would it be possible for you to *listen for a moment?*
Would you mind *stopping that noise?*
Are you sure you should *work that much?*
Are you trying to make a fool out of me?
(Why) can't you *stop talking for a moment?*
Must you *make such a noise?*

Die vorwurfsvolle Frage richten Sie in der Regel an **anwesende Gesprächspartner**. Sie kann **emotional verstärkt** werden und dann sehr verärgert klingen:

Why are you ***always*** *making fun of me?*
Why ***the hell*** *didn't you tell me earlier?*
How ***dare*** *you...?*
What ***on earth*** *are you doing there?*

Nobody Is Perfect

Trainer: **Couldn't you** have gone faster?
Jockey: Sure, but the rules say I must stay with the horse.

* * *

A young man bought a large grandfather clock at an auction. Struggling to carry it up the narrow staircase to his flat, he nearly struck his neighbour, an old lady, on the head.
"Idiot", she shrieked, "**why can't you** wear a normal wrist-watch like the rest of us?"

* * *

The upstairs tenant called to the downstairs tenant:
"**Must you** play the trumpet all day long? If you don't stop I'll go crazy!"
"**I'm afraid** it's too late", was the reply. "I stopped an hour ago."

* * *

At the most dramatic moment of the film the old man started grubbing around on the floor under the seats.
"**What on earth are you doing**?" hissed the angry woman next to him.
"Trying to find my toffee", whispered the man.
"**Can't you** wait till the end? You are ruining the film," snapped the woman.
"**I'm awfully sorry**", croaked the old boy, "**but** this toffee has got my false teeth stuck in it!"

* * *

A Glasgow wife arrived home from shopping and put six bottles of whisky and half a loaf of bread on the table.
Her husband saw this and shouted at her angrily:
"**What in the Lord's name** did you bring all that bread for, woman?"

Kritisieren und kritisiert werden

3. Seinem Ärger Luft machen

In Situationen, in denen Sie nichts oder nichts mehr verlieren können, ist das "Dampf ablassen" Gebot der psychischen Hygiene. Sie sagen, was Sie denken. Die sprachliche Ohrfeige, die Sie austeilen möchten, kann die **Form des Ausrufs oder Befehls** annehmen.

Ausrufe:

Look at *all that mess!*
How *stupid (silly, mean)* ***of you!***
How could you!
Shame on you!
What *a shame!* ***What*** *a nuisance!*
What a fool you are!
You are *making a fool of yourself!*
If you had only *followed my advice!*

Befehle, Anweisungen:

Don't be *silly!* ***Don't be*** *such a fool.*
Behave yourself.
You should / ought to be / *ashamed.*

Und mit **einfachen Aussagesätzen** läßt sich trefflich über abwesende Personen herziehen:

Peter is not a frank and open character.
That's disgusting. He is a peculiar person.
I'm getting tired of his unreliability.
The trouble with Paul is that he drinks too much.

Nobody Is Perfect

Office manager: **Look at all this** dust on this desk! It looks as if it hasn't been cleaned for months.
Cleaning lady: **Don't blame me, sir**. I've only been here a week.

* * *

Father: Oh Paul! **How silly of you**! You brought me the wrong boots. **Can't you see that** one of them is black and the other brown?
Son: Yes, Dad. But your other pair is just the same.

* * *

A little Scottish boy burst into the house and shouted: "Daddy, Daddy, today I ran home behind the bus and saved ten pence."
"**What a fool you are**!" cried his father. "You could have run behind a taxi and saved two pounds."

* * *

Mother: **You ought to be ashamed of yourself, Eddie! You've been** fighting **again**! And you've lost your front tooth!
Eddie: No, I haven't. It's in my pocket.

* * *

Angry employer: **You should have been** here at nine o'clock.
Young employee: Why? What happened?

* * *

Robert: **Behave yourself** and **stop acting like a fool**.
René: I'm not acting.

* * *

Vicar: **You should not** fight, **my boy**. **You ought to** love your enemy.
Boy: But he's not my enemy. He's my brother.

Kritisieren und kritisiert werden

4. Sich zur Wehr setzen

Der normale Bürger überspringe diesen Abschnitt. Es geht hier um Schach- und Sprachzüge, mit denen Juristen, Politiker (und Ehefrauen?) auf Kritik zu reagieren pflegen, nämlich mit **Gegen- und Entlastungsangriffen** oder einer **Retourkutsche** wie dieser:

Lady Astor:	Winston, you are impossible! If I were your wife I'd put poison into your tea.
Churchill:	**If you were my wife**, I'd drink it.

Die vorwurfsvolle Gegenfrage:

Can you prove that?
Are you suggesting that I am *a liar?*
What do you mean by *that?*
If that's the case, then please tell me why you...?
Are you accusing me of *having broken that vase?*
You don't really mean *that, do you?*
You don't really mean to say *that I am...?*
I really don't see why *I have to...?*
Excuse me, but what is the point of *doing that?*
But can't you see *...?*

Abstreiten:

We are not to blame.	***It wasn't me.***
It's not really my fault.	***Don't blame me.***
You have no reason to...	***Why do you always pick on me?***
It wasn't me, I assure you.	***Don't pass the buck to me.***

Nobody Is Perfect

Father: **Don't you know that** reaching over the table for cake is bad manners? **Haven't you got** a tongue?
Son: Yes, but my arms are longer.

* * *

"**Don't you think you should** change the water in the goldfish bowl?"
"**Why should I**? They haven't drunk the first lot yet."

* * *

René: Are you trying to make a fool of me?
Robert: **Sorry. I really don't mean to. Why should I** try to change nature?

* * *

"Peter!"
"What, Mum!"
"Are you spitting in the fish bowl?"
"**No, Mum, but I'm coming pretty close**."

* * *

In a railway carriage an elderly lady was annoyed by a little boy who kept sniffing. At last she said: "**Haven't you got a handkerchief**?" "Yes", said the boy, "but my **Mum wouldn't like me to lend it to a stranger**."

* * *

"Waiter! **What is this** fly **doing** in my soup?"
"**Hum... Looks like breast-stroke, doesn't it**?"

* * *

"**How dare you** belch in front of my wife?"
"**Sorry. I didn't know** it was her turn."

* * *

"Waiter! This egg is bad."
"**Don't blame me**. I only lay the table."

Kritisieren und kritisiert werden

5. Eingeständnis und Entschuldigung

Mit folgenden Strategien des Eingeständnisses und glaubhaft gespielter Zerknirschung kommen Sie einer Kritik zuvor.

Die präventive Entschuldigung:

I'm not quite sure how to put this, but I'm afraid I'*ve smashed up your car.*
I'm afraid I seem to have *run over your dog.*
I'm afraid I've got something to tell you.
I've got a bit of an apology to make.

Der gebildete Mensch vergibt mit folgenden Redemitteln:

I quite understand. Please don't worry! These things happen.
That's all right. Never mind! It doesn't matter!
Don't worry about it! We all make mistakes, don't we?

Entschuldigungen nach der Panne:

I can't tell you how (awfully) sorry I am.
I'm ever so sorry.
I do apologize. I apologize for doing... (formal)
I'd like to apologize. It won't happen again.
I regret that I was unable to... (im Brief)
Sorry, I didn't mean to *annoy you / want to hurt you.*
I just don't know what to *say.*
I had no intention of *hurting you / your feelings.*

Nobody Is Perfect

She (in public telephone box): Hello, darling. Is that you? **I'm sorry to trouble you, but** we've got a little problem with my car. I...
He: What's wrong with the car, darling?
She: **I don't know how to explain this, darling, but** the motor won't start. There seems to be some water in the carburettor.
He: Don't cry. I'll be with you in a minute. By the way, where is the car?
She: In the Thames, near Greenwich.

* * *

"Waiter! **Look at that!** You've brought me a lobster with only one claw."
"**I'm ever so sorry, sir, but** it lost its claw in a fight."
"**Never mind!** Take it away and bring me the winner."

* * *

A tourist saw an advertisement for a restaurant which claimed that any dish requested could be served. The man decided to test this restaurant. He entered and ordered an elephant on toast. The waiter took the order and went away into the kitchen. A few minutes later, he returned and said calmly: "**We do apologize, sir, but** we have run out of bread."

* * *

Boss: **Why the hell are you** late again this morning?
Typist: **I'm extremely sorry, sir.** I overslept. **It won't happen again.**
Boss: You mean, you sleep at home as well as here?

* * *

"Waiter! **What is this fly doing in my soup?**"
"**I'm most awfully sorry, sir.** Would you prefer it to be served separately?"

Nobody Is Perfect

Little Mary was on a train with her mother when suddenly she started to whisper in her mother's ear.
"Mary", said her mother sharply, "**how many times have I told you it's impolite to whisper**. If you have anything to say, say it aloud."
"Alright," shouted Mary, "why has that man got such big ears?"

* * *

Hedgehog finding himself on top of a scrubbing brush:
"**We all make mistakes, don't we**?"

* * *

The best of Murphy's "Table of Handy Office Excuses" (to be introduced by: Excuse me but...):

1. ...that's the way we've always done it.
2. ...I didn't know you were in a hurry for it.
3. ...that's not my department.
4. ...that's his job, not mine.
5. ...we don't make many mistakes.
6. ...I didn't think it was very important.
7. ...I wasn't hired to do that.

Arthur Bloch

* * *

Just to be complete: The most efficient sexual excuses: These excuses should be introduced by "I'm afraid, but...; I'm awfully sorry, but...; Sorry darling...; or in rare cases by: Sorry girls (boys), but...

1. ...I've got a headache.
2. ...not here, darling. Somebody might see us.
3. ...what if the kids hear us?
4. ...I'm just not in the right mood.
5. ...I've just come home from the hairdresser's.
6. ...not without dinner, a drink and a cigarette first.

Test
Nobody Is Perfect

1. Choose the most appropriate response.

René: I wanted to thank you for lending me your car.
Robert: No problem.
René: Unfortunately I had a small accident. You will need a new door.
Robert: ______________?
René: I didn't want to spoil your dinner.

a) Was it really necessary to do that?
b) What a fool you are!
c) Excuse me, but what was the point of doing that?
d) Why the hell didn't you tell me earlier?

2. Fit in an appropriate function or phrase.

There was a cowboy in a bar boasting that he was the fastest gun in the West. A week later he limped into the bar; he was covered in bandages. His friend didn't know what to say. "______________ but what on earth happened to you?" – "I got shot." – "But you said you were the fastest gun in the West." – "I am," replied the cowboy. "I was on holiday in the East when it happened."

3. Give the most appropriate function for the German in the brackets.

Ross: *(Entschuldigen Sie die Störung)* but is this train running on time?
Neal: No, it's running on rails.

4. What would you say if . . .

you were sitting at a table in a restaurant eating your steak and suddenly your neighbour began to smoke a cigar?

1) Don't be such a fool!
b) I'm afraid I've got something to tell you.
c) How could you!
d) I've got a bit of a problem here.

Just For Fun

Young Ronny applied to a big advertising company for a part-time job. The personnel manager, wanting to test Ronny asked, “My boy, what would you do with a million pounds?”
Ronny: “Well, sir, I wasn’t expecting that much at the beginning.”

* * *

Glen, leaving for his office, was asked by his middle-aged, far from attractive wife:
“Glen darling, what would you do if you came home and found me in bed with another man?”
Glen, angrily: “I’d break his white stick over his head and then shoot his guide dog.”

* * *

Client: I’d have to be an idiot to buy stock in your company.
Tycoon: Well, how many shares do you want?

* * *

McTavish catches his wife in bed with John. He goes for a gun to shoot his rival. “Don’t shoot before you have heard my story,” she cried. Remember that fur coat I told you was a cheap imitation? It was real. Johnny bought it for me. Remember the expensive television set. I told you I won it in a raffle. Johnny paid for it. And you remember our last holiday in Switzerland – well it was...”
MacTavish interrupted her shouting on top of his voice: “Quick. Cover him up. He might catch a cold.”

* * *

Graffito:
Living on earth is expensive but it
includes a free trip round the sun.

Being Astonished, Being Surprised

Das darf nicht wahr sein!

Seiner Überraschung, seinem Erstaunen oder Zweifel Luft zu machen ist nicht nur ein Gebot seelischer Hygiene. Der sprachliche Umgang mit diesen Gefühlen kann beim Anbahnen von Zweierbeziehungen sogar ausschlaggebend für eine harmonische Zukunft sein. So dürfen Sie einer Dame, die Ihnen ihr Alter gesteht, zwar immer mit anerkennendem Staunen, nie aber mit gehobener Augenbraue und einem freundlichen "*Really*!" begegnen. Denn dies ist die typisch britische Reaktion auf Versprechungen von Vertretern und Politikern, ein *understatement* für "*You are a damned liar*." So glatt ist das englische Parkett.

Wie bei vielen *speech functions* kommt es sehr auf Mimik und Tonfall an, welche Wirkung Sie mit diesen Redemitteln erzielen.

Das darf nicht wahr sein!

1. Erstaunen äußern

Reiseberichte und Krankheitsgeschichten begleitet der geschulte Zuhörer mit Ausrufen höflichen Staunens. Er ermuntert die Erzähler auf diese Weise zur weiteren Ausschmückung ihrer Geschichten.

Well, well, well!	Hört!Hört!/ Na sowas!
Marvellous!	Großartig! Wunderbar!
It's amazing.	Das ist erstaunlich.
Incredible!	Unglaublich!
Unbelievable!	Unglaublich!
Fancy that!	Stellen Sie sich vor!
Would you believe it!	Was Sie nicht sagen!
You do surprise me.	Sie überraschen mich.
You don't say.	Was Sie nicht sagen!
That beats everything!	Das ist einmalig/unerhört!
I'm amazed to hear/see...	Ich bin erstaunt...
I'll be damned! (fam.)	Mir fehlen die Worte!

Diese Varianten der *'question tags'* drücken **ungläubiges Staunen** aus:

René has got a medal for self-discipline.	***He hasn't!***
He is going to marry a second time.	***He isn't!***
And he gave up drinking last month.	***He didn't!***

Being Astonished, Being Surprised

One female student to the girl sitting next to her:
"What strikes me about our new tutor is how well he dresses."
Second girl: "Yes, **it's amazing**! And how quickly, too."

* * *

The young lady drove up to the curb when the policeman told her sternly that she had been doing seventy-five miles per hour.
"**Would you believe it**!" she exclaimed. "And I'm just learning to drive."

* * *

An American woman on a holiday trip to Germany stood in awe in front of an enormous tree in the hotel park. "**Oh, marvellous**! **What a** proud and ancient oak tree you are! If you could only speak, what would you say?"
"Well, madam", said one of the gardeners, "it would probably say: 'Pardon me, madam, but I'm an elm.'"

* * *

McTurd was stopped by a beggar who asked him for some money. "I haven't eaten for over four days," he said gloomily.
"**You don't say. What** self-control!" exclaimed McTurd. "But you shouldn't exaggerate."

* * *

Hein was shopping in New York and saw a $ 2000 toupé of luxuriant hair in a shop window. "**That beats everything**!" he said to his wife. "They can make hair grow on that thing but not on your head."

* * *

After a pub crawl René was staggering back to his hotel, drunk as usual. He was watching a man enter the revolving door. As the door swung around, a pretty girl stepped out.
"**I'll be damned**", he muttered.

Being Astonished, Being Surprised

The attractive teenage girl was driving home late at night after visiting her boyfriend's house. She was stopped by a policeman and asked to take the breath test. The girl blew into the breathalizer which instantly changed colour.
"Well, now", said the policeman. "You've had a stiff one tonight, miss."
"**Unbelievable**!" exclaimed the girl. "Does that show, too?"

* * *

A husband and his wife believed in reincarnation. They agreed that when one of them died, the other would reach him through a medium. He died first. Two months later she went to the medium and told her that she would like to talk to her husband. The medium said it could be arranged. After a few soundings of bells and horns, the wife heard his voice.
"Bill," she cried, "is that you? **Marvellous**! Tell me, how is everything up there where you are?"
He replied, "You ought to see the beautiful pink cows, the glorious mauve cows, and beautiful black and white cows."
"**Fancy that**!" she exclaimed, "but is that all you have to talk to me about... beautiful cows?"
"Listen, darling, I am a bull on a farm in Montana."

Herbert Hershfield

* * *

Bob: Have you got any plans for tonight?
René: Yes, I'm going to play chess with my dog.
Bob: **It's amazing** – it must be a really intelligent animal.
René: Not really. I won three games to two last night.

* * *

A visitor at an asylum saw one of the loonies pushing a wheelbarrow upside down. "That's not the way to push that thing", the visitor explained. "You've got it upside down."
"**Oh, have I**?" answered the lunatic. "I used to push it the other way round, but then they put sand in it."

Being Astonished, Being Surprised

One absent-minded professor said to another professor, "**I'm amazed to see how much** you've changed your outward appearance. You've put on weight, you wear glasses and your hair has turned blond. What has happened to you, Professor Greenstein?"
"But I'm not Professor Greenstein," protested the other.
"**You don't say**! You've even changed your name!"

* * *

McTavish had just returned from a holiday in Arizona. "I was surrounded by wild looking Indians. Indians in front of me, Indians behind me, Indians all around me. I was frightened stiff."
"**Jesus**!" said McNab. "What did you do?"
"What could I do?" said McTavish with a deep sigh. "I had to buy a blanket."

* * *

René and Anne were dining in an expensive Paris restaurant when he noticed a fly in his soup. He demanded to see the manager, and being proud of his knowledge of the French language he pointed to the plate and said: "Monsieur, ***un mouche***!"
The manager looked at the soup and said: "Non, monsieur, c'est ***une mouche***."
"**Good Lord**!" exclaimed René. "**What good eyesight**! I couldn't see the difference."

* * *

"What a terrible bump on your head! What did that?"
"Tomatoes."
"**Heaven**! How could tomatoes cause a huge bump like that?"
"They were in a tin."

* * *

Son: How do I find the highest common denominator?
Father: **Good gracious**! Haven't they found that yet? They were looking for it when I was at school.

Das darf nicht wahr sein!

Eine beliebte Form des Überrascht- und Erstauntseins ist in allen Religionen die Anrufung der Gottheiten und Heiligen, wobei aus Pietät der Mißbrauch des Namens Gottes durch Ersatzwörter wie ***dear, gosh*** vermieden werden kann.

My God!	***Good grief!***
Good Lord!	***Good gracious!***
Jesus!	***Man alive!***
Good heavens!	***Oh dear!***
Heavens!	***Gosh!***

Auf solche Ausrufe antworten Sie ebenfalls mit einer Anleihe aus der Bibel: ***It's the gospel truth*** – Es ist so sicher wie das Amen in der Kirche.

Unterbrechen Sie den Redefluß Ihres Partners mit erstaunten Zwischenfragen. Nach der zu erwartenden Reaktion wird er in seiner Story fortfahren.

Erstaunte Frage	**Zu erwartende Reaktion**
Really? / Is that so?	***It's a fact.***
Not really?	***It's just as I'm telling you.***
Are you sure?	***I'm absolutely sure about it.***
Are you joking?	***No, I'm not, I assure you.***
Are you serious?	***I'm dead serious.***
Can you believe it?	***There's no doubt about it.***
Would you believe it?	***You can believe me.***

Being Astonished, Being Surprised

A tourist from Texas was watching the fishermen at a French seaside resort. "What are those things on the beach?" he asked one of the fishermen. – "Lobster pots," was the reply. "**Good gracious**!" exclaimed the Texan. "**That beats everything**! You've trained the lobsters to sit on those pots?"

* * *

An Irishman got a job at an observatory. During his first night's duty he paused to watch a learned professor who was peering through an immense telescope. Just then a star fell. – "**Man alive**!" exclaimed the astonished Irishman. "You're a fine shot."

* * *

President Bush: I just bought my wife a Rembrandt.
Helmut Kohl: **Really?** Mine doesn't like sports cars.

* * *

René: A funny thing happened to my mother in Glasgow.
Bob: **Are you sure**? I thought you were born in Nottingham.

* * *

She: I celebrated my 28th birthday yesterday?
He: **Not really**! Again?

* * *

Eric: I come from a very old military family. One of my ancestors fell at Waterloo.
Ernie: **Really**?
Eric: **It's a fact**! Someone pushed him off platform nine.

E. Morecombe and Ernie Wise

* * *

René: I used to be a tough fighter when I was younger. I could lick a man with one hand.
Bob: **Not really**?
René: **It's just as I'm telling you**. Unfortunately, I could never find a man with one hand who wanted to fight.

Das darf nicht wahr sein!

2. Ungläubiges Staunen äußern

Der Erzählkunst mancher Vertreter des Weidwerks und der Seefahrt wird oft zu Unrecht ungläubiges Staunen entgegengebracht. Ihnen seien einige Wendungen zur Beteuerung ihrer Wahrheitsliebe an die Hand gegeben:

Angriff	Verteidigung
Tell it to the marines!	***But it's really true.***
Do you expect me to believe that?	***You can take my word for it.***
Are you kidding?	***No, I'm not, honestly.***
Are you pulling my leg?	***I wouldn't dare.***
A likely story!	***I'm ready to take an oath on it / to swear to it.***
Get away with you!	***It's the gospel truth.***

* * *

Prince Charles: *This is a dreadful golf course. Just look at the state of it!*

Body guard: *This isn't the course, Your Majesty. We left that half an hour ago.*

Prince Charles: ***Are you kidding?***

Body guard: ***I wouldn't dare****, Your Majesty. But I'm afraid* ***it's a fact.***

Prince Charles: ***Really****? Is that why you keep looking at your watch?*

Body guard: *This isn't a watch – this is a compass!*

Being Astonished, Being Surprised

A Bavarian on a visit to Paris decided to send a surprise birthday gift to his wife at home in Munich. He rang INTERBIRD and told them to send her a parrot that spoke seven languages. When he arrived home the following day, he found that she had plucked and roasted the bird.

"**Good Lord**!" he shouted at her. "That bird spoke seven languages."

"**Are you pulling my leg**? Why didn't he say something before I put him in the oven?"

* * *

While on holiday in Cairo McTavish was amazed to see so many stray dogs and cats running around. "What do those animals live on?" he asked his guide.

"Scraps of food thrown away," answered the guide.

"**Get away**!" marvelled McTavish. "Funny that we've no animals like that in Scotland."

* * *

Snake-charmer: Careful with my suitcase, porter. It contains a rare ten-foot snake.

Porter: **Go and tell it to the marines**, ma'am. I know that snakes don't have any feet.

* * *

Bob: You've a girl in a million, René.

René: I know – I just wish she was normal like everyone else. For twelve years, Bob, I didn't know what sex was.

Bob: **Get away! Do you expect me to believe that?**

René: **You can take my word for it.** But when I was thirteen...

* * *

Bob: Our dog is just like one of the family.

René: **You don't say.** Which one?

Test
Being Astonished, Being Surprised

1. Choose the most appropriate response.

_____________ how just enough things seem to happen to fill the newspapers every day?

a) Fancy that | *b) I'm amazed to hear*
c) I'll be damned | *d) Isn't it amazing*

2. Fit in an appropriate function or phrase.

Anne: Hey, Susan. I hear there is a husband-swopping party down the road on Sunday. Shall we go?

Susan: _______________? Who'd have mine?

3. Match up the sentences in the two columns.

René says:	Robert replies:
1. Neal has won a prize for politeness.	a) He's like that. It's true enough.
2. The Berlin Wall has come down.	b) Oh dear, did she?
3. What strikes me about Neal is the importance money has in his life.	c) It's the gospel truth.
4. No, I can't believe that.	d) He hasn't!
5. And then she had an accident on her bike.	e) Good heavens. I'd never have believed it.

4. Give the most appropriate function for the German in the brackets.

A mother, worried about her teenage daughter, sat her down and had a long talk about the bees and the birds.
"*(Tatsächlich? Stimmt das?)*" marvelled the girl. "It's a fact", replied the mother. "Well," said the girl thoughtfully, "then no wonder I'm pregnant."

Showing Doubt And Uncertainty

Ungewißheit und Zweifel

Hier lernen Sie, mit Unwissenheit, Ungewißheit, Vermutungen und Zweifeln sprachlich umzugehen. Dieses Kapitel sei all jenen gewidmet, die mit den überlegenen, von diesen Schwächen verschonten Zeitgenossen leben müssen.

Ungewißheit und Zweifel

1. Wie sprechen wir über unsere Unwissenheit?

Wenn ein Philosoph sagen kann 'Ich weiß, daß ich nichts weiß', dann dürfen auch wir Unwissenheit offen eingestehen. Das ist weniger anstrengend, als zu raten und zu spekulieren. Darüber hinaus geben Sie dem Partner ein Gefühl der Überlegenheit, was durchaus zu Ihrem Vorteil sein kann.

I'm afraid, I don't know.
I've never heard of it.
I have no idea.
I haven't a clue.
I haven't the slightest idea.
I haven't the faintest idea.
I haven't the foggiest notion.
Ask me another!
That's beyond me.
I can't see / understand why...

Achten Sie auf die Intonation!

Wie bei den meisten Sprechfunktionen macht der Ton nicht nur die Musik, sondern verändert auch die Bedeutung des Gesagten.

1. Freundlicher Ton	= bitte belehren Sie mich
2. Kühler Ton	= behalten Sie Ihre Weisheit für sich
3. Unfreundlicher Ton	= wechseln wir schnell das Thema

Showing Doubt And Uncertainty

"Mum, how do the elephants make love?"
"**I've no idea**, son – your father is a Smith."

* * *

"What time is it when two elephants sit on your fence?"
"**Ask me another**."
"Well, it's time to buy a new one."

* * *

"How do you get four elephants in a taxi?"
"**I haven't the faintest idea**."
"Two in the front and two in the back."

* * *

John: I wonder which family the whale belongs to.
Bob: **I don't know**. In any case, no family in our neighbourhood has got one.

* * *

The British sense of tradition:
I was travelling to Canterbury by train and when it stopped at a small station a man in uniform came out with a little hammer and tapped all the wheels.
"Why are you doing that?" I asked him.
"**I haven't the foggiest notion**, but I have been doing this for twenty years," said the man.

* * *

Two Sicilian mafiosi armed with machine guns were waiting for the new judge of Palermo to assassinate him.
One said, "We can't miss him. He walks by here every day by himself at noon." Twelve o'clock came, no judge showed up . . . twelve-thirty . . . one o'clock . . . no judge.
Finally the other said, "**I can't understand this**. He comes by here every day at twelve noon sharp. I hope nothing has happened to him."

Ungewißheit und Zweifel

Unwissenheit ist kein Makel, sondern ein Informationsdefizit, das sich leicht beheben läßt. Folgende Sprechfunktionen signalisieren Wißbegierde und Lernbereitschaft.

I'd like to know.
I wonder + Fragewort.
I wish I knew + Fragewort.
I wish I knew.
If I only knew.
If only I knew.
Could you explain to me + Fragewort?

Vorsicht ist besser als Nachsicht. Wer rechtzeitig die richtigen Fragen gestellt hat, bedarf der Redemittel der späten Reue nicht.

I wish I'd known.
If only I'd known.
Had I known…
I didn't realize that…

Showing Doubt And Uncertainty

René: **I'd like to know how** long a human being is able to live without a brain.
Anne: How old are you?

* * *

Variety is the spice of life:

Two married couples who had met at a party decided to exchange partners in order to make life more interesting. The next morning the two husbands met at breakfast. "Well, I quite enjoyed that," said the first. "So did I," agreed the second, "**I wonder how** the girls got on."

* * *

"**I wonder why** the people who need money most, are always the very ones who never seem to have it."

* * *

"**I wish I knew**," said Molly, "**why** the milk company is complaining about a shortage of glass milk bottles. I've got thousands of them at home."

* * *

Bob: **If only I knew whether** to be a painter or a poet.
René: I think you should be a poet.
Bob: You mean you've read one of my poems?
René: No. But I've seen one of your paintings.

* * *

"**Could you explain to me** why people say 'Amen' and not 'Awomen'?" Bobby asked. – "That's obvious," his friend Ronny replied. "It's because we sing hymns and not hers, silly."

* * *

Nicolai Ceaucesco wanting to know how he stood with his people hired an American pollster. Within a week the expert reported to the 'titan of titans': "Ninety-nine percent of the people love and admire you. But **I wish I knew why** I only kept running into that other one percent."

Ungewißheit und Zweifel

Fehler, die Sie aus Unwissenheit begehen, können Sie oft mit mangelhafter Information entschuldigen und so den Schwarzen Peter weiterschieben. Deshalb werden Ihnen die folgenden Redemittel nützlich sein, um Vorwürfe zurückzuweisen.

I'm afraid I wasn't informed.
How shall / should I know?
How could I have known?
How was I to know?
It's news to me.
I don't follow you.

2. Wie man Unsicherheit zu erkennen gibt

Je nach Situation können Sie mit den nächsten Redemitteln Unsicherheit, Zögern oder Ihre abwartende Haltung zu erkennen geben.

I'm not certain.
I can't say for certain.
I couldn't really say if…
I'm not quite certain.
I'm not sure.
I'm not a 100 % sure.
I'm in two minds about it.

Showing Doubt And Uncertainty

In a restaurant:
"Waiter, waiter, what's this in my soup?"
"**How should I know**? All insects look the same to me."

* * *

On my last visit to Ireland I was not sure whether I was on the right road. I asked a farmer on a hay wagon, "Which way is it to Limerick, please?"
"**Don't know**," the farmer answered.
"Well then, which way is it to Cork?" I asked.
"**I haven't a clue**".
I was getting angry. "Don't you know anything?"
"Well," said the farmer, "I know my way, I'm not lost."

* * *

The Jewish bookmaker, after a day of bad luck at the race course entered a kosher restaurant and ordered a steak. When it arrived he looked at it doubtfully and asked the waiter: "**Are you sure** this steak is kosher?"
"It should be. It won three races for Lord Rothshild."

* * *

Graffito:
Only the Pope and I are infallible . . .
but **I'm not too certain** about him.

* * *

"Darling, now that we're married will you tell me, am I the first woman in your life you ever took to bed?"
"Well, let me see? **I'm not a hundred percent sure**. Were you in Nottingham twenty years ago?"

* * *

Teacher: Why did the Stone Age people draw pictures of rhinoceroses and hippopotamuses on cave walls?
Pupil: **I'm not sure**. **Perhaps** they didn't know how to spell them.

Ungewißheit und Zweifel

Geben Sie Ihrer persönlichen Unsicherheit einen Hauch philosophischer Gelassenheit. Denn was ist in dieser Welt schon sicher.

One never knows. ***Maybe, maybe not.*** ***God only knows.***	***You can never tell.*** ***It might or might not work.*** ***Who knows?***

In vielen Situationen ist es sinnvoll, sich nicht sofort festzulegen, sondern Zeit zum Nachdenken zu gewinnen.

I'm in two minds about it. ***I don't know what to think of it.***	***I'll have to think about it.*** ***I haven't come to a conclusion yet.***

Auch wenn Sie Ihrer Sache sicher sind, ist es klug, die Möglichkeit eines Irrtums nicht kategorisch auszuschließen.

If I remember correctly… ***As far as I remember/know…*** ***For all I know…*** ***It might be wrong but…***	***If my memory doesn't fail me…*** ***If I'm not mistaken…*** ***I may be wrong but…*** ***It can/could be true, but…***

Showing Doubt And Uncertainty

Bob and René were going home one night, when they saw a young couple making love in a park.
René: I didn't have sex with my wife before I got married, did you?
Bob: **Maybe, maybe not**. What was her maiden name?

* * *

"Grandpa, what's the reason for your old age?"
"Well, **God only knows**. Maybe because I was born such a long time ago."

* * *

Two cats were looking at a bird in a cage.
"I don't believe it's a canary," said the first cat. "A canary isn't green."
"**You never know**," said the second. "**Maybe** it's not ripe yet."

* * *

"Tell me doctor, how long do I have to live?"
"**You can never tell**, but if I were you I wouldn't start watching any TV serials."

* * *

"Doctor, **are you a hundred percent certain** that this medicine will cure my insomnia?"
"It must", the doctor replied. "**As far as I remember**, nobody ever came back for more."

* * *

"Will television ever replace newspapers?" –
"It might or it might not. **Who knows**?"
"Well, I do. Have you ever tried to kill flies with a television?"

* * *

Uncle: And what are you giving your brother for his birthday?
Maggie: **You can never tell**. Last year I gave him the measles.

Ungewißheit und Zweifel

3. Spekulationen und Mutmaßungen

Wenn Sie in Diskussionen nicht selbst harte Fakten auf den Tisch legen können, sind Sie deshalb noch lange nicht zum Schweigen verurteilt. Verleihen Sie den Argumenten allzu gewisser Partner mit den Redemitteln des Annehmens und Vermutens den Hauch des Ungewissen. Und dies geht so:

Could it be that *these statistics are incomplete?*
Might it be possible that *these figures are wrong?*
Am I right in assuming that *the bank will help us?*
Supposing *these figures are correct.*
I assume *our competitor hasn't a similar product.*
I suppose *we should try it.*
I suspect *that there is no market for your product.*
I reckon *the managing director is right.*
It seems to me that…
I bet *it will be a success.*
Just suppose *we ran out of money.*
Just imagine *that there was a strike.*
Presumably / Perhaps / Probably…
I presume…
I believe…

Showing Doubt And Uncertainty

Thatcher: My great-grandfather fought against Napoleon, my grandfather fought against the Massai and my father fought against the Germans.
Kinnock: **It seems to me that** your family isn't able to get along with anybody.

* * *

Thatcher: **I suppose** this portrait is what you call modern art.
Artist: Actually, it isn't a portrait. It's a mirror.

* * *

"I washed him and then he died," explained Bob to the vet who he had called in to investigate into the death of his dog. "**I bet it was** the soap you used," said the vet. – "**Perhaps** it was," said Bob, "or **could it be that** it was the washing machine he didn't like?"

* * *

At an auction Lord Gray wanted to buy a rare exotic bird. After almost an hour of hard bidding he obtained the bird at an exorbitant price.
"**I assume** this bird can talk," he said to the auctioneer.
"Talk!" exclaimed the man. "Who do you think has been bidding against you for the past fifteen minutes?"

* * *

A candidate for the Polish Communist party was undergoing an examination. "Comrade," he was asked, "**supposing** you were left two million zloty, what would you do?"
"Well, **I suppose** I'd give one million zloty to the party and keep the other million for myself." – "Very good. Now, **just imagine** you had two houses." – "I would give one house to the party and keep the other for myself." – "Very good. Now **supposing** you had two pairs of trousers." – There was a long pause and then the candidate said weakly, "Comrade, **I don't know**." – "Why not?" – "Well, you see, I have two pairs of trousers."

Ungewißheit und Zweifel

4. Zweifel äußern – Redemittel für Skeptiker

Die Übergänge von der Mutmaßung zum Zweifel sind oft fließend und hängen von Situation und Tonfall ab. Folgende Aufhänger des Zweifelns geben Ihnen den Anschein des vorsichtigen Denkers – auch wenn Sie über keine eigenen Argumente verfügen.

I can't help wondering if…
I really wonder if…
I really ask myself if…
***What if** these figures are wrong?*

Berechtigte Bedenken und Zweifel leiten Sie so ein:

I wonder.	***Are you sure?***
I've some doubt about it.	***I doubt it.***
I rather doubt that…	***It's rather unlikely.***
I can't imagine that.	***I don't believe…***
I should say it might be but…	***I don't suppose** you could lend me some money.*
I wouldn't bet on it.	***I wouldn't rely on it.***
Are you joking?	***Are you pulling my leg?***
You must be joking.	***You don't mean to say that…***

Showing Doubt And Uncertainty

"Hmm – a salary increase, eh?" said the managing director. "**I suppose** you've often wondered what you'd do if you had my kind of income, haven't you?"
"No," said the assistant. "But **I've frequently wondered** what you would do if you had mine."

* * *

An extremely beautiful young patient was visited in her room by the professor. As he lifted her gown to take a look, he asked her: "**I can't help wondering** if my staff are taking good care of you."
"They certainly are," said the girl. "You're the forty-eighth doctor who has examined me this morning."

* * *

Anne: Father, has mother told you? I'm afraid I'm pregnant.
Father: **Are you sure** it's yours?

* * *

A father talking to his baby: "Whose little baby are you? Whose little baby are you? Whose little..."
At that moment the kid looked up and said: "**So you're beginning to wonder**, too?"

* * *

The vicar was explaining the difference between certainty and faith to his congregation.
"In the front row", he said, "we've Mr Bosewell with his wife and her four children. Now, she knows they are her children. He hopes they are his children, but **he wouldn't bet on** it. That's faith."

* * *

When Bob saw the tombstone with the inscription:
'Here lies the body of a politician and an honest man', he thought to himself: "**I doubt it. I can't imagine** that there is enough space for two men."

Showing Doubt And Uncertainty

An East-Friesian at the library:

Heintje: I'd like something to read.

Librarian: **I suppose** you want something light.

Heintje: It doesn't matter. I've got my tractor outside.

* * *

Teacher: Now, Ronny, if Bob gave you a dog, and Dave gave you a dog, how many would you have?

Ronny: Four, of course.

Teacher: Now, Ronny, think hard. **Are you sure that** you would have four dogs, if Bob gave you one and Anne gave you one?

Ronny: Four of course. You see, I've already got two dogs.

* * *

"Do you know what happened when the Scottish football captain lent the referee a penny to toss for the ends?"
"**No, I haven't a clue**."
"He demanded the ref's whistle as security."

* * *

"Why do white sheep eat more than black sheep?"
"**I haven't the slightest idea**."
"Because there are more white sheep than black sheep."

* * *

Inscription on a gravestone at Anworth, Grote House of Fleet.

Stop passer-by as you pass by.
As you are now so once was I,
As I am now so you will be.
So be prepared to follow me.

Someone had scribbled beneath:

To follow you I'd be content
If I only knew which way you went.

Showing Doubt And Uncertainty

Dan was waiting at Shannon airport. "I've come to meet my brother," he said to his neighbour, "it's his first trip home from America in forty years." – "**It's rather unlikely that** you will recognize him," said his neighbour.
"I'm sure I won't," said Dan, "after all these years."
"**And I don't suppose** he will recognize you."
"Of course he will," said Dan, "sure I haven't been away at all."

* * *

Conversation between two Irish from Cork:
Paddy: Was your latest child a boy or a girl, Sally?
Sally: Have a guess, Paddy.
Paddy: **How shall I know**? Was it a boy?
Sally: No, guess again.
Paddy: It was a girl.
Sally: Oh, somebody must have told you.

* * *

Tourist: Can you tell me if this path will take me to the Huber Alm?
Bavarian: **I wouldn't rely on it**, sir. You'll have to go by yourself.

* * *

He: I heard a new joke the other day.
She: Oh, no, not again. You told it yesterday.
He: **I wonder**. It's very funny.
She: Then you didn't.

* * *

Probably no man has got so much conversation out of an operation as Adam did.

* * *

American: In Florida we always have fantastic weather.
Englishman: Well, **it's beyond me** how to start a conversation with a stranger then.

Test
Showing Doubt And Uncertainty

1. Fit in an appropriate function or phrase.

René: Do you know what the traffic warden had on his bread?
Bob: ________
René: Traffic jam!

2. Match up the sentences in the two columns.

René says:	Robert replies:
1. How long will it take to pay for your house?	a) Yes, you'll have to think it over.
2. We are in two minds about buying the windmill.	b) Well, you're right there.
3. I wouldn't bet on him passing his driving test.	c) Well, it's too late now.
4. I wish I'd known the police were waiting.	d) God knows!
5. That Neal got married was news to me.	e) Yes, it was a bit of a shock.

3. Give the most appropriate function for the German in the brackets.

Once Mrs Thatcher was giving a speech to a crowd of rather aggressive onlookers in a rural area. Suddenly a large cabbage was thrown at her. It just missed her ear but she didn't even blink. Her comment: "I *(nehme an)*, one of my opponents has lost his head."

4. What would you say if...

somebody told you that Mrs. Thatcher had invested a billion pounds in the National Health Service?

a) I bet it will be a success. *b) You must be joking.*
c) I'm not 100% sure. *d) Would you believe it?*

Showing Likes And Preferences

Vorliebe und Gefallen

Bekanntlich neigt der nüchterne Brite dazu, seine Gestimmtheit durch *understatements* zu verschleiern. Wo der Südländer sich seiner Geliebten zu Füßen wirft und tränenreiche Liebesschwüre leistet, sagt der Brite zu seiner Britin *"You know, I don't object to you at all"*, und sie bestellen gemeinsam das Aufgebot. Diese feinen Unterschiede sind gerade bei den Redemitteln der Vorliebe und des Gefallens zu berücksichtigen.

Vorliebe und Gefallen

1. Die Basisverben *prefer* und *like*

Mit diesen Verben meistern Sie fast alle Grundsituationen:

I like *beer.*	Ich mag Bier.
I prefer *beer* ***to*** *wine.*	Mir ist Bier lieber als Wein.

2. Abgeschwächte Variationen von *preference*

Da Sie als Leser dieses Buches nicht zu den schlichten Gemütern gehören, werden Sie schon bald das Bedürfnis verspüren, den Ausdruck Ihrer Vorliebe Partnern und Situationen anzupassen.

I'm quite in favour of *living together.*
I tend to favour *long socks.*
It would be better if *we didn't tell the boss.*
Perhaps we ought to *compromise* ***rather than*** *go to court.*

3. Direkte Formen von *preference*

I like *mineral water* ***better than*** *wine.*
I'd rather *die* ***than*** *tell a lie.*
I'd sooner *wait for the film than read the book.*
I'd rather you / I'd sooner you didn't wear skirts, Bob.

Showing Likes And Preferences

Sometimes statistics have a double meaning:
28% of women **prefer** men with fat legs
14% of women **prefer** men with thin legs.
The other 58% **like** something in between.

* * *

At one of the very expensive colleges in Switzerland where American millionaires send their children between divorce and marriage a little boy turned to another and asked
"**How do you like** your new father?"
"Oh, **I preferred** our third dad. The new one is a pain in the neck."
"Yes, isn't he? We had him two years ago."

* * *

"**What I like about** Hollywood is that one can get along with two words of English – swell and lousy."

Vicky Baum (attributed)

* * *

"Waiter! There's a fly in my soup."
"**Would you prefer** it to be served separately?"

* * *

Some doctors tell their patients the bad news man to man;
others **prefer** to send the bill by mail.

* * *

Patient: Doctor, does it take long to pull my bad tooth?
Dentist: Only two seconds.
Patient: And how much will it cost to have this done?
Dentist: Fifty dollars.
Patient: For only two seconds?
Dentist: I could pull it out more slowly, **if you prefer**.

Showing Likes And Preferences

Psychiatrist: What is your problem?
Patient: **I prefer** long socks to short socks.
Psychiatrist: So what? Lots of people do. Personally, **I tend to favour** long socks, too.
Patient: Really? Well, that's a relief! **How do you like** yours – fried or boiled?

* * *

Bob, Ross and René were discussing how they would like to die.
"**I'd like to** die peacefully in my cottage in Spain while drinking wine and listening to Bach," said René.
"**I'd rather** die after planting a flag on top of Mount Everest," said Ross.
"**I'd prefer to** die in bed," said Bob, "shot by a jealous husband."

* * *

"Mum, now that I'm fifteen, can I wear high-heeled shoes and a miniskirt?"
"**I'd rather you** didn't, Charles."

* * *

"Waiter! Is this whisky pure?"
"As pure as the girl of your dreams."
"Oh! Then **I'd rather not** have it."

* * *

Herr Häberli: There's no country like ours. **I'd rather be buried in Switzerland than** live in England.
Mr McTavish: I don't know. Take away your mountains and your valleys and your lakes, and what have you got left?

Showing Likes And Preferences

Irish Dan was lying on his death bed and asked for the protestant Reverend Ian Paisley because he wanted to convert to Protestantism. "But why?" asked his astonished friends. "You've been a good catholic all your life."
"Well," said the dying man, "**I'd sooner** it was one of them who died instead of a catholic."

* * *

John was in the army but ran away in the heat of the battle and was charged with desertion.
At the trial he defended himself by saying, "**I'd sooner** be a coward for five minutes than a corpse for the rest of my life."

* * *

Bob: Have you read the Bible?
René: No, **I'd rather** wait for the film.

* * *

Little Ronny was staying with his grandmother in the Black Forest for his holidays.
"**Would you like** to see the cuckoo come out of the cuckoo clock?" asked his grandmother.
"**I'd rather** see Grandpa come out of the grandfather clock", said Ronny.

* * *

An elderly manager to the new secretary:
"**I must say I quite like you**, Miss Austeen. You seem to be one in a million."
"So are your chances", replied the girl sharply.

Vorliebe und Gefallen

4. Allgemeine Ausdrücke des Gefallens

Beachten Sie, daß ein Gesprächspartner des anderen Geschlechts Ihr harmloses ***"I must say, Miss Robinson, I quite like you"*** als *understatement* für eine heiße Liebeserklärung auffassen könnte.

I quite like *Italian food.*
I enjoy *talking to intelligent people.*
I'm keen on *pop music.*
I'm rather keen on *playing tennis.*
I'm rather fond of *talking about my travels.*
I fancy *French wines.*

5. Ausdruck starken Gefallens

What I like best *about girls is . . .*
I really like *my boss.*
I'm really into *. . .*
I love *Italian food.*
I'm all in favour of *capitalism.*
He's really carried away with *. . .*
I'm dead keen on *. . .*
I'm crazy about *. . .*
I adore Margaret Thatcher.

6. Ausrufe des Entzückens

Great!	***Incredible!***
Super!	***Marvellous!***
Fantastic!	***Wow!***

Showing Likes And Preferences

René: You always seem to be talking to yourself. It's not very polite, if you ask me.
Bob: It's because **I enjoy** talking to an intelligent person and **I like to** hear an intelligent person answer.

* * *

Bob on holiday in France sent the following postcard to his psychiatrist:
"**I'm crazy** about France. **I enjoy** the food. I'm having a wonderful time. Why?"

* * *

Girl: Perhaps **you would like to** see where I got sunburnt.
Boy: Oh, yes please. **I'd love to.**
Girl: Here's a photo of Brighton beach.

* * *

Old lady: Mr Policeman, I want to report a rape.
Policeman: Yes, madam, when did it happen?
Old lady: In August 1947.
Policeman: In 1947! Why are you reporting that now?
Old lady: **I'm so fond of** talking about it once in a good while.

* * *

Jesus **loves** Black and White.
But he **prefers** Johnny Walker.

* * *

Last words of a British minister:
I like to do my job
It makes me feel so good
I enjoy doing as Thatcher thinks I should.
I adore her as **I adore** the Queen
I listen to what she has to say
I even like the men in white
That are taking me away.

Showing Likes And Preferences

Bob: Do you remember that holiday we had last year in Italy?
René: Sure.
Bob: And you remember that Italian student I was going out with?
René: Which one?
Bob: The one I said I couldn't live without. **I got really carried away by** her.
René: Oh, that one. A stunning girl she was. What about her?
Bob: I've forgotten her name.

* * *

"All the things **I'm really crazy about** are either immoral, illegal or fattening."

Alexander Woollcott

* * *

Bob: How do you like your change from salesman to teacher?
René: Fine. The pay is regular and the hours are satisfactory. But **what I like best is** that the pupil is always wrong.

* * *

Bob: **Which** of your relations **do you like best**?
René: Sex.

* * *

"We like you so much better than the last doctor," one patient of a home for mentally ill people told a new member of the staff.
"That's very kind of you, but how do you know? I've only just arrived."
"Well, they all say that you are more like one of us."

Test
Showing Likes and Preferemes

1. Choose the most appropriate response.

René: I ____________ the wife a cup of tea in my pyjamas.
Bob: That's why your pyjamas are always so soggy.

a) prefer to take *b) 'm all for taking*
c) would be better to take *d) fancy taking*

2. Fit in an appropriate function or phrase.

Mother cannibal to child:
"I' ____________ speak with somebody in your mouth."

3. Match up the sentences in the two columns.

René says:	Robert replies:
1. Wow, that was the best film I've ever seen.	a) I think you're right. I do it, too.
2. I fancy dark-skinned girls.	b) I'm doing my best.
3. I tend to talk too much.	c) How do you suggest I do that?
4. I'd sooner you saved your money.	d) Don't exaggerate.
5. Perhaps you ought to learn to relax.	e) They're my cup of tea, too.

4. Give the most appropriate function for the German in the brackets.

John: *(Wie war)* your holiday in Australia?
Neal: *(Herrlich!)* It's got everything for the family – a lot of pubs for me, shops for the wife, beaches for the kids, sharks for the mother-in-law.

5. What would you say if...

Boris Becker had just played a perfect winning stroke?

a) I'm all in favour of him. *b) I'd rather he won.*
c) He's really carried away. *d) Incredible!*

And Now Sit Back And Smile

René: Darling, if we get married do you think you will be able to live on my income?

Anne: Of course, darling. But what are you going to live on?

* * *

A young couple on their honeymoon. The first night, she went up to their room and locked the door, so nervous was she. He was still at the bar drinking whisky to overcome his excitement. She fell asleep and was wakened by frantic knocking at the door.

"I am not going to open the door," she cried. "I know what you are knocking for."

"But wouldn't you like to know what I am knocking with?" came the desperate reply.

* * *

Bob: Can you guarantee, doctor, that if I give up drinking, smoking and sex, I will live longer?

Doctor: No, but it will seem longer.

* * *

It's terrible to bring up a family today, considering the price of beer and cigarettes.

Woody Allen

* * *

René: Last night Annette asked me to marry her and make her happy.

Bob: Which did you choose?

* * *

Eve was the most frustrated of women: she couldn't tell Adam what a wonderful man her first husband was.

We Are Not Pleased

Enttäuschung und Mißfallen

Wir hoffen, daß Sie im Ausland nie in Lebenslagen geraten, in denen Sie von diesen Redemitteln Gebrauch machen müssen. Doch ist es immer noch besser, seinem Mißfallen Luft zu machen, als es hinunterzuschlucken.

Enttäuschung und Mißfallen

1. Wie man seine Enttäuschung kundtut

Wie bei allen Emotionen so werden auch diese Redemittel durch Gestik, Tonfall und Lautstärke abgeschwächt oder verstärkt.

Resignation, leichte Enttäuschung

It's been one of those days.
I'd hoped for more.
It's a bit disappointing that…
I'm rather disappointed that…
I somehow thought that…

Enttäuschung und Verärgerung

They've really let us down.
I've never been so disappointed.
It's a great shame that…
You've really stuck a knife in my back.
You couldn't have let me down more.

* * *

Denis Thatcher was reading the Times and was deeply shocked when he saw that most of the shares his wife had advised him to buy had fallen sharply. He rushed into her office and shouted: "My God, ***this time you've really stuck a knife into my back****…" Margaret Thatcher interrupted him sharply: "How many times must I tell you, Denis, that when nobody is present you may call me Margaret."*

We Are Not Pleased

An old Indian chief was in the dentist's chair. He was faced with a painful extraction.
"**It's been one of those days**," he sighed. "Will it hurt much?"
"Let's put it this way," smiled the dentist, "you won't be handing down any oral traditions for a while."

* * *

Ronny came home crying his eyes out. His mother told him:
"Such a big boy. **I'm rather disappointed** in you crying. What's the matter?"
"Dad and I were fishing when he hooked a really big one. Then the line snapped."
"Okay, **it's a bit disappointing** but a big boy like you shouldn't be crying. You should have laughed."
Ronny cried even louder: "That's exactly what I did."

* * *

Father: How was your first day in school?
Boy: Well, **I'd hoped for more**. I can't read, I can't write, and the teacher won't even let me talk.

* * *

Neal: **I've never been so disappointed in my life**. My wife is lying to me. She said she spent the night with Gaby.
Ross: How do you know she was lying?
Neal: Because I spent the night with Gaby.

* * *

"Why are you in such a hurry?"
"I'm on the way to the doctor. **I don't like** the looks of my husband."
"Oh! Then I'll come with you – **I hate** the sight of mine, too."

Enttäuschung und Mißfallen

2. Wie man Mißfallen und Abneigung ausdrückt

Folgende Ausdrücke des blanken Mißfallens sind sparsam zu verwenden:

Einfaches Mißfallen

I don't like *his looks.*
I'm not very keen on *alcohol.*
I don't fancy *going to operas.*
I'm not sure I'd like *to meet her again.*

Starke Abneigung

I dislike him intensely
I can't stand *rock music.*
I can't bear *that man any longer.*
I hate *going to school.*
I detest *Greek food.*
I loathe *liars and politicians.*

Wie beim Vorwurf oder der Kritik äußert der höfliche Mensch sein Mißfallen nicht ohne ein sprachliches Vorspiel:

Please forgive me for saying so, but I'm not too keen on *garlic.*
I hope you don't mind me saying this but I'd rather not *stay.*
I'm afraid I've got something to tell you. I can't love *you.*
I'm afraid I'm not quite sure how to put this, but *I must ask you to stop coming to our house.*

We Are Not Pleased

Hotel manager: Well, sir, I hope you enjoyed your stay with us.
Guest, looking at the bill: Yes, but **I don't like the idea** of leaving the place so soon after I've practically bought it.

* * *

"It's not that **I'm not keen on boxing**. It's that I wish I had a low enough I. Q. to enjoy it."

* * *

Boss: **I can't bear** 'Yes' men. When I say 'no' I want them to say 'no', too.

* * *

Girl: Stop! **I hate that.**
Boy: No!
Girl: Well, at least I resisted.

* * *

Graffito:
I hate graffiti.
Written beneath:
I'm not very keen on Italian food either.

* * *

John Doorbar went into a pub in Belfast and started chatting with the locals. After a while the conversation turned to politics. And just to please the Irish he said:
"Well, you know, **I can't stand** Maggie Thatcher, either. Her face looks like a sheep's head." Half an hour later he came round, bruised and beaten up.
"What was that for?" he asked. "I thought everyone here in Northern Ireland **detested** Mrs Thatcher. Is this Tory territory or what?"
"No," said the barkeeper, "sheep territory".

Test
We Are Not Pleased

1. Choose the most appropriate response.

Bob: My wife used to say, "_________ lips that touch alcohol. So I haven't kissed her for eight years."

a) I'm a bit disappointed that *b) I don't fancy*
c) I loathe *d) I'm not very keen on...*

2. Fit in an appropriate function or phrase.

Ronny: _________ going to school, and I have to stay here until I'm sixteen.

Teacher: I know how you feel – I've to stay here until I'm sixty-five.

3. Match up the sentences in the two columns.

René says:	Robert replies:
1. I'm not keen on dancing.	a) No, I hate it, too.
2. I can't stand arguing.	b) You can't make a silk purse out of a sow's ear.
3. We'd hoped for more from Uschi.	c) I don't care for it either.
4. You've really stuck a knife in his back.	d) You have to take the rough with smooth.
5. It's been one of those days.	e) I know. I didn't mean to.

4. Give the most appropriate function for the German in the brackets.

"I *(hasse)* housework: You make the beds, you do the dishes – and six months later you have to start all over again." Joan Rivers

5. What would you say if...

your friend telephones you at the last minute to say he cannot go away with you for the weekend?

a) You've really stuck a knife in my back. *b) I can't bear it.*
c) It's a bit disappointing. *d) I'm not very keen on it.*

They say that if a man runs after money . . .

... he is money mad. If he keeps it, he is a capitalist. If he spends it, he is a playboy. If he doesn't get it, he is a good-for-nothing. If he doesn't try to get it, he has no ambition. If he gets it without working for it, he is a parasite. And if he gets it after a lifetime of long and hard work, people will call him a fool who never got anything out of life. But you can learn a lot from a fool like that.

Wörterverzeichnis

999	Notruf in England
absent	abwesend
absent-minded	zerstreut
acceptable	annehmbar
accompany	begleiten
account	Rechnung, Konto
accuse someone	jemanden beschuldigen
achievement	Leistung
actually	eigentlich
add	hinzufügen
admire	bewundern
admit something	etwas zugeben
adore someone	jemanden sehr mögen, verehren
advance someone money	jemandem Geld vorstrecken
advert	Annonce
advertisement	Annonce
advice	Rat
advise someone / something	jemandem / etwas raten
affirmative answer	positive, bejahte Frage
afford: I can't afford it	ich kann es mir nicht leisten
agree	einer Meinung, einverstanden sein
agreement	Übereinstimmung
alike: look alike	sich ähnlich sehen
all the same	dennoch
allow someone something	jemandem etwas erlauben
along: go along with sth.	einverstanden sein mit
although	obwohl
ambassador	Botschafter
ambulance	Krankenwagen
ancestor	Ahn, Vorfahre
ancient	sehr alt
anguish	Schmerz, Pein, Angst
announce	an- / verkünden
annoyed	verärgert
anxiety	Angst
apologise for something	sich für etwas entschuldigen

apology	Entschuldigung
appear	(er-)scheinen
appear in court	vor Gericht erscheinen
appendix	Blinddarm
applicant	Bewerber
appoint someone	jemanden ernennen
appointment	Termin, Verabredung
approach someone	sich jem. nähern, jem. ansprechen
appropriate	angemessen, passend
approve of something	etwas billigen
argue with someone	mit jemandem streiten
ashamed: be ashamed	sich schämen
ask me another	frage mich etwas Leichteres
ass	Esel, Hintern
assistant	Verkäufer
assume that ...	vermuten, annehmen, daß ...
assure: I assure you ...	Ich versichere Ihnen ...
asylum	Irrenanstalt
attend a party	eine Party besuchen
attendant	Wärter, Aufsicht
audience	Publikum
awake	wach
awe	Ehrfurcht
back on one's back	wieder auf dem Rücken (liegen)
bandage	Verband
bang on	genau richtig
bark	bellen, Rinde
Bavarian	Bayer
beans	Bohnen
bear up!	Kopf hoch!
bear: I can't bear him	Ich kann ihn nicht ausstehen
beat someone up	jemanden verprügeln
beggar	Bettler
behave yourself!	benimm dich!
belch	rülpsen
belief	Glaube
beneath	darunter
bet on something	auf etwas wetten, setzen
bewilderment	Verwirrung, Verblüffung

beyond: that's beyond me	das ist mir zu hoch/schwer
bid against someone	gegen jemand bieten
bill	Rechnung
birth-control	Geburtenkontrolle
birth-notice	Geburtsanzeige
blackmail	Erpressung
blame someone	jemandem die Schuld geben, tadeln
blame: I'm not to blame	Ich bin nicht schuld
blanket	Decke
blindfold someone	jemandem die Augen verbinden
blink	blinzeln, mit der Wimper zucken
blow off	weggeblasen, weggeweht werden
bluntly: to put it bluntly	um es ungeschminkt zu sagen
boast	angeben, prahlen
boil an egg	ein Ei kochen
bookmaker	Buchmacher (Wettbüro)
boring	langweilig
bother	sich Sorgen machen
bother someone	jemanden belästigen, stören
bra	Büstenhalter
bracket	Klammer (...)
brains	Hirn, Grips
brainstorm	Gedankenblitz, verrückter Einfall
breast-stroke	Brustschwimmen
breath test	Alkoholtest
breathalizer	"Röhrchen", Alkoholtestgerät
breed	hier: sich fortpflanzen
bride	Braut
bridegroom	Bräutigam
bright	hell, klug, intelligent
brighten up the house	Licht ins Haus bringen
bring something up	erwähnen, zur Sprache bringen
broke	pleite
brothel	Bordell
bruised	zerschunden
buck: pass the buck to someone	jemandem den Schwarzen Peter zuschieben
bump	Beule

burglar	Einbrecher
burgle a house	in ein Haus einbrechen
burst into (an office)	hinein stürmen
bury someone	jemanden begraben
butcher	Metzger
button	Knopf
by all means	bitte sehr, aber gewiß
by the way	übrigens
cabbage	Kohl(kopf)
caller	Anrufer
calling card	Visitenkarte
calm down	beruhige dich
campaign for, against	kämpfen für, gegen
cancel	stornieren, absagen
candle	Kerze
carburettor	Vergaser
care a damn about	sich den Teufel scheren um
care for something	etwas mögen, sich etwas machen aus
carriage	Eisenbahnwagen
carry away	begeistern, hinreißen
catch fire	Feuer fangen, brennen
catch a train	einen Zug erreichen
cause	Grund, Ursache, Anlaß
cause for concern	Grund zur Sorge
cause pollution	Umweltverschmutzung verursachen
cave	Höhle
century	Jahrhundert
certain	sicher, gewiß
certainty	Gewißheit
chairperson	Vorsitzende/r
chamber of horrors	Gruselkabinett
championship	Turnier, Meisterschaft
change	hier: Kleingeld
change one's ways	seinen Lebenswandel ändern
chap	Bursche
charge someone	jemanden beschuldigen
chase one's hat	seinem Hut nachlaufen
chat with someone	mit jemandem plaudern

cheat on the taxes	Steuern hinterziehen
check a file	in einer Akte nachsehen
check-up	Untersuchung
cheek	Backe
chef	hier: Küchenchef
chip in	sich einschalten (in Gespräche)
chocolate bar	Schokoladenriegel
choice	Wahl, Auswahl
chore	Arbeit, schwierige Aufgabe
citizen	Bürger
claim something	etwas behaupten
claw	Zange (des Hummers)
cleanliness	Sauberkeit
close enough	hier: ganz gut erraten
clue: I haven't a clue	ich habe keine Ahnung
coated in	überzogen, mit einer Schicht aus
coax someone to do	jem. gut zureden etwas zu tun
cobs: I'm sweating cobs	ich schwitze vor Angst
coffin	Sarg
coincidence	zufälliges Zusammentreffen
collection plate	Teller für die Kollekte
column	(Druck-)Spalte, Kolumne
come off it!	Hören Sie doch auf!
come round	wieder zu sich kommen
comfort someone	jemanden trösten
comforting	beruhigend
commence again	wieder anfangen
comment	Bemerkung, Kommentar
commit a crime	ein Verbrechen begehen
common denominator	der gemeinsame Nenner
complain	sich beklagen, beschweren
complaint	Beschwerde
compulsory	verpflichtend, obligatorisch
concern	Sorge, Besorgnis
concerned: as far as I'm ≈	was mich anbelangt
conclude	schließen, abschließend bemerken
conclusion	Entschluß, Schlußfolgerung
confess	gestehen, beichten
congregation	Gemeinde, Versammlung
conscious of something	etwas bemerken

consider	in Erwägung ziehen, überlegen
consider important	für wichtig halten
console someone	jemanden trösten
contain whisk(e)y	Whisky enthalten
contamination	Verunreinigung, Verseuchung
content	zufrieden
continental	vom Kontinent; kontinental
contraceptive	Verhütungsmittel
convert to	sich bekehren zu, übertreten zu
convict someone	überführen, schuldig erklären
convinced	überzeugt
cooperation	Zusammenarbeit
copulate	sich paaren, kopulieren
corpse	Leiche
cough	Husten
cough politely	höflich husten
count on someone	sich verlassen auf, rechnen mit
coupon	Lottoschein
court	Gericht
coward	Feigling
crazy	verrückt
cremate someone	jemanden feuerbestatten
croak	krächzen
cross the lines	die Schienen überqueren
cross: lets cross our fingers	toi, toi, toi; drücken wir die Daumen
cruise	Kreuzfahrt
cuddle	schmusen
culprit	Übeltäter, Schurke
cup: it's not my cup of tea	das ist nicht mein Geschmack
curb	Randstein
cushion	Kissen, Polster
cut out Fridays	Freitage streichen, auslassen
daisy	Gänseblümchen
dare	wagen
dare: don't you dare . . .	untersteh dich und . . .
dare: how dare you . . . ?	Wie kannst du es wagen . . . ?
darts	Wurfpfeilspiel
dearly: love dearly	von Herzen lieben
decision	Entschluß, Entscheidung

deed	Tat
defend oneself	sich verteidigen
defendant	Angeklagte(r)
degrees in psychology	Diplome in Psychologie
depression	Depression; Tiefdruckgebiet
desertion	Fahnenflucht
detest something	etwas verabscheuen
device	Vorrichtung
diet	Diät
differ	anderer Meinung sein
disagree	anderer Meinung sein
disappointed	enttäuscht
disappointment	Enttäuschung
disapproval	Mißbilligung
disease	Krankheit
disgraceful: it's ≈	es ist eine Schande
disgusting	ekelhaft, schrecklich
dishes	Geschirr
dispel the clouds	die Wolken vertreiben, auflösen
distinctly	deutlich, klar
distrustful	mißtrauisch
disturbing	beunruhigend
divine left (breast)	eine göttliche linke Brust
divine right	göttliches Recht
divorce	Scheidung
divorce someone	sich von jemandem scheiden lassen
doctrine of predestination	Lehre von der Vorherbestimmung
donkey	Esel
"Double Trouble"	etwa: „Doppelter Ärger"
doubt	Zweifel; zweifeln
down in the mouth	deprimiert
draught	(Luft-) Zug
draw a meeting to an end	eine Konferenz schließen
draw to a close	zu Ende gehen
dreadful	schrecklich
driving instructor	Fahrlehrer
due: be due to	hier: sollen müssen
dull	langweilig

early bird: the ≈ catches the worm	Morgenstund hat Gold im Mund
earring	Ohrring
East-Friesian	Ostfriese
economics	Wirtschaftswissenschaften
editor	Herausgeber
efficient	wirksam; tüchtig
effort	Mühe, Anstrengung
elm	Ulme
embarrassed	verwirrt, peinlich berührt
embarrassed silence	peinliche Stille
empty-handed	mit leeren Händen
enjoyable	angenehm
enjoy doing something	etwas gerne tun
enjoy something	sich einer Sache erfreuen
enquiry	Anfrage
entitled: be entitled to	das Recht auf... haben
escape	entkommen
eschatological	(Jesus hat das auch nicht gewußt)
even numbers	gerade Zahlen
exaggerate	übertreiben
exaggeration	Übertreibung
examination	Untersuchung
except for	außer, abgesehen von
except for the fact that...	außer der Tatsache, daß...
excited	aufgeregt
exclaim	ausrufen
executive	leitender Angestellter
exhausted	erschöpft
exorbitant prices	unverschämte, maßlose Preise
expensive	teuer
extra hours	Überstunden
extraction	Zahnziehen
eye-shadow	Liedschatten
fact	Tatsache
fail someone	jemanden im Stich lassen
fail to do something	etwas unterlassen, nicht schaffen
failure	Versager; Mißerfolg
faint: not the faintest idea	nicht die leiseste Ahnung
faith	Glaube

false teeth	Gebiß
familiar	gewohnt, vertraut
famous	berühmt
fancy that	Stell dir vor...
fancy: I fancy Italian food	ich mag italienische Küche
fatal	tödlich
fattening	dick machend
fault	(Charakter-)Fehler
favour	Gefallen
fed up: I'm fed up with	Ich habe die Nase voll
fellow passenger	Mitreisender
female	weiblich
fence	Zaun
fiancée	Verlobte
file	Akte
file in	antreten (zur Arbeit)
fine shot	guter Schütze
firm belief	fester Glaube
fit as a fiddle	munter wie ein Fisch im Wasser
fit like a glove	wie angegossen sitzen
fitting-room	Ankleidekabine
flu	Grippe
foggy: to have not the foggiest notion	nicht den leisesten Schimmer haben
fond: I'm fond of wine	ich mag Wein sehr gerne
fool	Dummkopf, Narr
fool someone	jemanden täuschen, hereinlegen
foreign affairs	Außenpolitik
Foreign Legion	Fremdenlegion
foreign relations	Außenpolitik, Verkehr m. d. Ausland
foreigner	Ausländer
forgiveness	Vergebung
frankly	offen gesagt
fraternity	Zunft, Gilde
frequent	häufig
fried	gebraten
frog	Frosch
fruits of love	Früchte, Freuden der Liebe
full marks	ausgezeichnet, große Klasse
function	hier: Redemittel

funeral	Beerdigung
furiously	wütend
gadget	technische Spielerei
galley	Küche, Kombüse
gamble	spielen (um Geld)
garlic	Knoblauch
generous	großzügig
genuine pigskin	echtes Schweinsleder
get along/on with	auskommen mit
get away	entkommen
get some exercise	sich körperlich bewegen
gift	Geschenk, Gabe
giggle	kichern
give in	nachgeben
gloomy	düster, betrübt, traurig
go ahead	nur zu
good health!	Zum Wohl! Auf Ihre Gesundheit!
gorge	Schlucht
gospel: it's the gospel truth	so sicher wie das Amen in der Kirche
grab someone	jemanden packen
grain	Korn
grateful	dankbar
growl	knurren
grub around the floor	auf dem Boden herumstöbern
guess	raten
guidance	Führung
guide	Führer
guide dog	Blindenhund
guilty	schuldig
habit	Gewohnheit
hair: keep your hair on	reg'dich nicht auf
hairstyle	Frisur
handle something	sich um etwas kümmern
handsome man	ein gutaussehender Mann
handy	praktisch
hang around the house	im Haus herumlungern
hang on a minute!	einen Augenblick mal!

head	Führer, Kopf
headmaster	Schulleiter
health	Gesundheit
heart condition	Herzkrankheit
heat	Hitze
hedgehog	Igel
height and length	Höhe und Länge
hen-pecked husband	ein Ehemann unter dem Pantoffel
here you are!	bitte sehr, hier bitte
heroic	mutig, tapfer
hesitate	zögern
high-heeled	mit hohen Absätzen
hippopotamus	Nilpferd
hiss	zischen
hit someone	jemanden schlagen, treffen
hole	Loch
honesty	Ehrlichkeit
honour	hier: beehren, die Ehre geben
hooligans	Rowdies, Randalierer
hop	hüpfen
host	Gastgeber
hostess	Gastgeberin
House of Commons	das britische Unterhaus
house-warming party	Einweihungsparty
hurt someone	jemanden verletzen
hurt, hurt, hurt	weh tun, schmerzen
husband-swopping party	Party, auf der man Ehemänner tauscht
hymn	Hymne (Wortspiel mit *him* und *her*)
hypochondria	eingebildete Krankheiten, Hypochondrie
hypochondriac	eingebildeter Kranke(r)
I. Q.	Intelligenzquotient
I'm broke	ich bin pleite
Ian Paisley	radikaler protestant. Pfarrer
imitate	nachahmen
immediately	sofort
impolite	unhöflich

improve	verbessern
in the nude	nackt, als Akt
include someone	jemanden mit einbeziehen
income	Einkommen
incomplete	unvollständig
increase	Zunahme, Erhöhung (Gehalt)
incredible	unglaublich
indigestion	Verdauungsstörung
infallible	unfehlbar
inherit	erben
insist on	bestehen auf
insomnia	Schlaflosigkeit
instant dislike	sofortige Abneigung
instantly	sofort
insurance	Versicherung
insure someone	jemanden versichern
insured	versichert
intercom	Bordsprechanlage
intern	Internist
interrupt someone	jemanden unterbrechen
introduce someone	jemanden vorstellen
introduce something	etwas einführen, einleiten
investigate into	Nachforschungen anstellen
involved: get involved	verwickelt, hineingezogen werden
iron rod	Eisenrute
jam	Marmelade
jealous	eifersüchtig
join someone	sich jemandem anschließen
join the army	zur Armee gehen
joke	Witz; Witze machen
jury	die Geschworenen
keen on	Wert legen auf
keen: I'm dead keen on ...	ich bin versessen auf ...
keep a stiff upper lip!	halt die Ohren steif!
Keep out!	Eintritt verboten!
keep someone in after school	jemanden nachsitzen lassen
keep your end up!	Nur Mut! Nicht verzagen! Kopf hoch!

Keep your hair on!	Verlier nicht die Nerven
kerygma	(Jesus hat es auch nicht gewußt)
kidding: are you kidding?	machst du Witze?
kids	Kinder
kilt	Schottenrock
knock at	anklopfen
knocking-off time	Feierabend, Ende des Arbeitstages
kosher	koscher
label	Schild, Preisschild
lane	Gasse
latest: the latest joke	der neuste Witz
lavatory	Toilette
law	Gesetz
lawn-mower	Rasenmäher
lawyer	Rechtsanwalt
lay an egg	ein Ei legen
lay the table	Tisch decken
lazy	faul
leave her alone!	lasse sie in Ruhe!
lecture	Vorlesung, Referat
legs: I'm on my last legs	ich pfeife auf dem letzten Loch
lemon	Zitrone
lengthways	der Länge nach
let someone down	jemanden im Stich lassen
let someone off easy	jem. billig davonkommen lassen
let's call it a day	genug für heute
let's cross our fingers!	drücken wir die Daumen
let's have a vote	stimmen wir ab
librarian	Bibliothekar
lick someone	jemanden besiegen
lifeguard	Bademeister, Rettungsschwimmer
light	leicht, heiter; Licht
likewise	gleichfalls, ebenso
limelight	Rampenlicht
limp	humpeln
lisp	lispeln
living: make a living	seinen Lebensunterhalt verdienen

loaf	Laib (Brot)
loan	Darlehen, Kredit
loathe something	etwas verabscheuen
lobster	Hummer
local	Einheimischer
look alike	gleich aussehen
looks	Aussehen, Mine
loony, lunatic	Irrer
loss	Verlust
lost: be lost	sich verirrt haben
lot	Portion, Lieferung
lousy	lausig, miserabel
lowest bidder	günstigster Anbieter
luxuriant	üppig
luxury liner	Luxusdampfer
maiden name	Mädchenname
mail	Post
make a point	etwas bemerken, dazu sagen
make up with someone	sich mit jemandem (wieder) vertragen
manners	Manieren
marines: tell it to the ≈	mach' das jemand anderem weis
marry someone	jemanden (ver-) heiraten
Mars	1. Planet, 2. Schokoladenriegel
marvel	staunen
marvellous	wunderbar
mat	Fußmatte
match up	zuordnen
maternity ward	Entbindungsstation
mauve	malvenfarben
mean: I didn't mean to	das habe ich nicht gewollt
measles	Masern
measure a flagpole	einen Fahnenmast ausmessen
meat	Fleisch
medal	Medaille, Orden
meek	sanftmütig, die Sanftmütigen
meet God	vor Gott treten
memorable	denkwürdig
memory	Gedächtnis
mentally ill	psychisch krank, geistesgestört

mention something	etwas erwähnen
mention: don't mention it	wörtl.: erwähnen Sie es nicht, keine Ursache
merger	Firmenzusammenschluß, Fusion
mess	Saustall, Durcheinander
meter (metre)	Meter
Middle East position	politische Lage im Nahen Osten
mind your head!	Paß auf deinen Kopf auf!
mind your language!	Sei vorsichtig, was du sagst.
mind your own business	kümmern Sie sich um Ihre eigenen Angelegenheiten
mind: be in two minds about	unentschlossen sein
mineral rights	die Schürfrechte
miracle	Wunder
mirror	Spiegel
miser	Geizkragen
mistake	Fehler
mistaken: if I'm not ≈	Wenn ich mich nicht irre
mistress	Geliebte
mood	Stimmung, Verfassung
moth	Motte
mouche (französisch)	Fliege
mousetrap	Mausefalle
MP	Member of Parliament, Abgeordneter
m.p.h.	miles per hour
mud pies	Kuchen aus Dreck, Matsch
mum	Mammie
mutter	murmeln
national security	nationale Sicherheit
native	Eingeborener
neck	Nacken
newly-wed	frisch verheiratet
nibble	knabbern, nagen
noise	Geräusch, Lärm
nude	nackt
nudity	Nacktheit
nuisance: what a nuisance!	wie ärgerlich!
nurse	Krankenschwester

oak	Eiche
oath	Eid
obituary column	Todesanzeigen
object to someone	etwas gegen jemanden haben
obligatory	verpflichtend, obligatorisch
observatory	Sternwarte
obtain	erlangen, erhalten
obvious	offensichtlich, klar
occasion; on the occasion of	Gelegenheit; anläßlich
off: take a day off	einen Tag frei nehmen
onion	Zwiebel
opening night	Premiere
operate on someone	jemanden operieren
operator	Telefonvermittlung, Amt
opinion	Meinung
opinion poll	Meinungsumfrage
opponent	Gegner
opportunity	Gelegenheit
oppose something	gegen etwas sein
optional	freiwillig, (aus-)wählbar
oral traditions	mündliche Überlieferung
ordinary clothes	gewöhnliche Kleider
orgasm	Orgasmus
other: the other day	neulich
ought: you ought to go	du solltest eigentlich gehen
outward appearance	äußere Erscheinung
overcoat	Mantel
overhear something	etwas mithören
oversleep	verschlafen
overstay one's welcome	länger bleiben, als dem Gastgeber lieb ist
overweight: be overweight	zu dick, schwer sein
pain	Schmerz
pain in the neck: to be a ≈	nervtötend, eine Nervensäge sein
painful	schmerzhaft, schmerzlich
painter	Maler
pale	blaß
parachute	Fallschirm
parrot	Papagei

pass a sentence	ein Urteil sprechen
pass away	sterben, verscheiden
pavement	Bürgersteig, Trottoir
peculiar	sonderbar, seltsam
peep into	hinein spähen, schauen
peer	spähen, gucken
percolator	Kaffeemaschine
perfect	vollkommen
perfect shape	ausgezeichnete Verfassung
perfection	Vollkommenheit
performance	Auf-, Vorführung; hier: Sitzung
perky	flott, forsch, frech
perky copulator (das Mädchen meinte percolator, s. o.)	ein flotter Partner für den Geschlechtsverkehr
permission	Erlaubnis
permit, allow	erlauben
petal	Blütenblatt
phrase	Redewendung
pick on someone	auf jemandem herumhacken
piece of advice	Ratschlag
pigskin	Schweinsleder
pinch someone	jemanden zwicken
pink	rosa
pink mice	rosa Mäuse
pint (of beer)	ca. ein halber Liter Bier
pity: it's a pity	es ist schade
pluck (a bird)	rupfen
pluck up one's courage	seinen Mut zusammennehmen
poison	Gift
pollster	Meinungsforscher
pollution	Umweltverschmutzung
pools	Toto
position	Stellung (beim Geschlechtsverkehr)
post a letter	einen Brief aufgeben
practise something	etwas üben
pray for	beten um
preacher	Pfarrer, Prediger
precisely	genau
prefer something	etwas vorziehen
preference	Vorliebe

pregnant	schwanger
prejudice	Vorurteil
prejudice someone	jemanden voreingenommen machen
prepared to	bereit zu
prescription	Rezept (von einem Arzt)
press-ups	Liegestützen
presume	vermuten, annehmen
pretend	so tun, als ob
prevent someone from doing	jemanden an etwas hindern
prevention	Vorbeugen
previous appointment	eine frühere Verabredung
printer	Drucker, Druckerei
prize chicken	preisgekröntes Huhn
procedure	Vorgehen, Methode
propose something	etwas vorschlagen
proud of	stolz auf
prove something	etwas beweisen
provoke someone	jemanden reizen, herausfordern
prudish	prüde
psychiatrist	Psychiater
pub crawl	Sauftour
pull faces at someone	jemandem Gesichter schneiden
pull someone's leg	sich über jemanden lustig machen
pull yourself together	reiß dich zusammen
purpose	Sinn, Zweck
purser	hier: Chef des Schiffspersonals
put someone down	kritisieren, schlecht reden über
put someone down	jemanden töten, beerdigen
put someone up	jemanden beherbergen, unterbringen
quarrel	streiten
rabbit	Kaninchen
raffle	Tombola
rails	Schienen, Geleise
raise one's finger	sich melden
raise one's glass	sein Glas erheben

raise someone's salary	jemandes Gehalt erhöhen
rape	Vergewaltigung
rather: I'd rather . . .	ich würde lieber; ich ziehe . . . vor
reason	Grund
receipt	Quittung
receptionist	Sprechstundenhilfe; Portier
recipe	(Koch-) Rezept
reckon	denken, meinen
recognize	wiedererkennen
recognize someone	jemanden wiedererkennen
recommend someone to do sth.	jemandem empfehlen, etwas zu tun
recover	sich erholen, genesen
recovery	Genesung
referee (ref)	Schiedsrichter
reflectively: study someone ≈	jemanden nachdenklich mustern
refund money	Geld zurückzahlen
refuse to do something	sich weigern, etwas zu tun
regret something	etwas bedauern
reincarnation	Wiedergeburt
relations	Beziehungen, Verkehr, Verwandte
relatives	Verwandte
relax	sich entspannen
relaxation	Entspannung
relief	Erleichterung
religious instructor	Religionslehrer
rely on	sich verlassen auf
remain seated	Platz behalten, sitzen bleiben
remark	eine Bemerkung machen
remarkable	bemerkenswert
remember something	sich an etwas erinnern
remind someone of	jemanden an etwas erinnern
remove something	etwas entfernen
remote	entfernt, entlegen
replace	ersetzen, vertreten,
reply	antworten; Antwort
request someone to do sth.	bitten, fordern, verlangen
resign	kündigen
resist	widerstehen, sich wehren
response	Antwort

rest in peace	ruhe in Frieden
retirement	Pensionierung
retort	erwidern
retraction	Gegendarstellung
retreat	sich zurückziehen; Rückzug
reverend	Pfarrer
revolving door	Drehtür
ridiculous!	lächerlich!
rise, rose, risen	sich erheben, aufstehen
rise: ask for a rise	um Gehaltserhöhung bitten
rotten/lousy: I feel rotten	ich fühle mich mies, miserabel
rough: take the rough with the smooth	die Dinge so nehmen, wie sie kommen
row	Streit
rubbish!	Quatsch, Unsinn!
rude	unhöflich
rule	regieren
run down	erschöpft, überarbeitet
run into someone	auf jemanden treffen
run out of something	etwas wird einem knapp
run over a dog	einen Hund überfahren
rural area	ländliche Gegend
rush someone to the hospital	jemanden schnellstens ins Krankenhaus bringen
rust	rosten; Rost
satisfactory	zufriedenstellend
sausage	Wurst
save time	Zeit sparen
saw	Säge; sägen
scared: be scared	Angst haben
scraps	Brocken, Fetzen, Stücke
scrawl	kritzeln
screw someone	hier: ins Bett gehen, schlafen mit
scribble	kritzeln
scrubbing brush	Schrubber
seagull	Möwe
seasick	seekrank
seaside resort	Badeort (am Meer)
second to none	einzigartig
security	Garantie, Sicherheit

sedative	Beruhigungsmittel
see someone home	jemanden nach Hause bringen
seen: have someone seen to	jemanden untersuchen lassen
sentence	Urteil
separately	getrennt, einzeln
serial	(Fernseh-) Serie
sermon	Predigt
servant	Bedienstete(r)
service	hier: Gottesdienst
sew, sow, sewn	nähen
séance	(spiritistische) Sitzung
shake	hier: zittern
shame someone	jemanden beschämen
share	Aktie
share someone's view	jemandes Meinung teilen
shark	Hai
shit	scheißen, Scheiße
shiver	zittern
shot	Schuß; Schütze
shove off!	hau(t) ab!
show someone out	jemanden hinausbegleiten
shriek	kreischen
sigh	seufzen
sight	Anblick
sights	Sehenswürdigkeiten
sign	Schild, Zeichen
sign in as...	sich einschreiben, sich anmelden als
signed	unterschrieben
silly	dumm, töricht
similar products	ähnliche Produkte
sincerely	aufrichtig
sinner	Sünder
sit-up	Rumpfbeuge (im Sitzen)
skin and bones	Haut und Knochen
skirt	Rock
skylight	Deckenfenster
slimy	schleimig
slope	Abhang
slow down	langsamer fahren
smart	schlau

smash up the car	das Auto zu Schrott fahren
smooth: take the rough with the smooth	die Dinge so nehmen, wie sie kommen
sneer	höhnen
sniff	schnüffeln, schnupfen
sob	schluchzen, weinen
sober	nüchtern
soggy	feucht
solve problems	Probleme lösen
sooner: I'd sooner...	ich würde lieber; ich ziehe... vor
sound unfriendly	unfreundlich klingen
space	Raum, Platz
spare bedroom	leeres, übriges Schlafzimmer
speak up	laut sprechen
specimen of urine	Urinprobe
speech	Rede; Sprache
speed	rasen, zu schnell fahren
speedy recovery	schnelle Genesung
spell a word	ein Wort buchstabieren
spice	Würze, Gewürz
spit out (spat, spat)	(aus-)spucken
splitting headache	rasende Kopfschmerzen
spoil something	etwas verderben
spring cleaning	Frühjahrsputz
squad	(Einsatz-) Kommando, Truppe
staff	Personal
stagger	schwanken, torkeln
stagger to one's feet	schwankend aufstehen
stagnant (statt pregnant)	träge (statt schwanger)
stake: be at stake	auf dem Spiel stehen
starve	verhungern
stay	Aufenthalt
sternly	ernst, streng
stiff: a stiff one	ein Steifer (Drink; das Mädchen dachte dabei aber an den Freund)
stock-taking	Inventur, Bestandsaufnahme machen
stomach	Magen
stomach trouble	Magenbeschwerden

Stone Age people	Steinzeitmenschen
stork	Storch
stray dogs	streunende Hunde
strength	Kraft, Stärke
strike, struck, struck	schlagen
strike: what strikes me about	was mir auffällt bei...
stroll in a park	in einem Park spazierengehen
stunning looking	phantastisch gutaussehend
sub-way ride	Fahrt mit der U-Bahn
successful	erfolgreich
suggest something	etwas vorschlagen, anregen
suitcase	Koffer
summons	Strafzettel
sunburn	Sonnenbrand
Sunday school teacher	Religionslehrer
supersonic airliner	Überschall-Passagierflugzeug
superstitious	abergläubisch
support someone	hier: jemanden ertragen
support something	etwas unterstützen
suppose something	annehmen, meinen, denken
supposed: I'm supposed to...	Ich soll...
supposing that...	angenommen; nehmen wir an, daß...
surgeon	Chirurg
surprise	überraschen; Überraschung
survive	überleben
suspect	Verdacht haben; Verdächtiger
suspicious	verdächtig; argwöhnisch
swallow	(ver-)schlucken
swamp	überschwemmen
swear words	Flüche
swear, swore, sworn	schwören, fluchen
swell	toll
switch someone on	ansprechen, anmachen
swop/swap	tauschen
sympathy	Mitgefühl, Beileid
tail	Schwanz
take a day off	einen Tag Urlaub nehmen
take stock	Inventur machen
tap	klopfen, abklopfen, untersuchen

tea: that's not my cup of tea	das ist nicht mein Fall, Geschmack
tear-stricken	tränenüberströmt
teetotal	abstinent
television set	Fernsehapparat
tenant	Mieter
tend to	neigen zu
tether: at the end of one's tether	am Ende seiner Kraft
thieve	hier: Räuber
third-rate	drittklassig
thorough	gründlich
throughout the performance	während der ganzen Sitzung
thy	dein/e/en; altmodisch für *your*
tide	Flut
tidy	ordentlich, sauber
tin	Konservendose
tombstone	Grabstein
tongue	Zunge
topless	oben ohne
top marks	beste Noten
tortoise	Schildkröte
Tory	Mitglied der Konservativen Partei
toss for the ends	die Seiten auslosen (b. Fußball)
totter	wackeln, zittern
traffic jam	Verkehrschaos (siehe auch *jam*)
traffic warden	Verkehrspolizist
tranquillizer	Beruhigungsmittel
trap one's finger	seinen Finger einklemmen
tread, trod, trodden	treten
treat someone	jemanden behandeln
trial	Verhör
tribe	Stamm
trip	stolpern
triplets	Drillinge
trouble	Schwierigkeiten, Ärger, Probleme
trouble someone	jemanden stören, belästigen
trumpet	Trompete
turkey	Truthahn
turn off the TV	den Fernseher ausschalten

turn out alright	gut ausgehen, in Ordnung gehen
turn: I don't know which way to turn	ich weiß nicht mehr ein noch aus
turn: it's her turn	sie ist an der Reihe
TV serials	Fernsehserien
twins	Zwillinge
ultimate meaning	der letzte Sinn
undergo examination	überprüft, untersucht werden
understatement	Untertreibung
undertaker	Bestattungsinstitut,-unternehmer
under the weather	mit den Nerven am Ende
underwear	Unterwäsche
uneventful	ereignislos
unlikely	unwahrscheinlich
unreliability	Unzuverlässigkeit
unusual	ungewöhnlich
upset drinks	Getränke umstoßen
upset (stomach)	durcheinander, nicht in Ordnung
usual	gewöhnlich
variety	Abwechslung
vegetable	Gemüse
vet	Tierarzt
vicar	Vikar, Pfarrer
vin rouge (französisch)	Rotwein
virtue	Tugend
volunteer	sich freiwillig melden
voter	Wähler
wait for ages	eine Ewigkeit warten
wallet	Brieftasche
wallpaper	Tapete
watch it!	Paß auf! Achtung! Vorsicht!
Watch your step!	Vorsicht Stufe!
ways: change one's ways	seinen Lebenswandel ändern
wealth	Wohlstand
wear lipstick	sich die Lippen schminken
wear: I'm the worse for the wear	Ich bin ziemlich fertig
weigh 75 kilos	75 Kilo wiegen

whale	Walfisch
wheelbarrow	Schubkarre
whether	ob
whisper	flüstern
whistle	Pfeife
widow	Witwe
wig	Perücke
wit	Geist, Witz
wit: I'm at my wit's end	Ich bin mit meinem Latein am Ende
with a rod of iron	hier: mit eiserner Faust
wording	Wortlaut
work camp	Arbeitslager
worry	sich Sorgen machen
worth knowing	wissenswert
wrap up the meeting	die Konferenz schließen
wristwatch	Armbanduhr
xerox something	etwas photokopieren
zloty	polnische Währung

Lösungen zu den Tests

(Es kann vorkommen, daß bei manchen Tests mehr als eine Lösungsmöglichkeit richtig ist)

Starting and Ending Conversations

1. d
2. 1d 2a 3b 4c 5e
3. We can wrap up this interview.
4. d

How are you?

1. c
2. You look the shadow of your former self.
3. 1e 2d 3a 4b 5c
4. I've got problems with my eyes.

Inviting and Being Invited

1. a
2. 1e 2a 3b 4c 5d
3. Why not use . . . ?
4. c

The Right Word at the Right Time

1. c
2. Congratulations
3. 1a 2b 3d 4e 5c
4. Good luck

Would you do me a Favour

1. c
2. I'm sorry to bother you
3. 1e 2d 3a 4b 5c
4. Would you be so kind as to…

I'm a bit worried…

1. b
2. 1d 2e 3a 4b 5c
3. I can't stand it anymore.
4. b

Don't Worry! Be Happy!

1. b
2. Take it easy
3. 1e 2a 3b 4d 5c
4. You shouldn't worry yourself about that.

Tell Them What You Think

1. b
2. 1b 2a 3c 4e 5d
3. I think
4. a

How To Agree With People

1. a
2. That's just what I was thinking
3. 1a 2d 3b 4c 5e
4. I quite agree

Disagreeing with People

1. d
2. I can't accept that
3. 1e 2b 3c 4d 5a
4. I'm not completely convinced

Granting Permission

1. b
2. Please, let me . . .
3. Do you mind if I/No, just go ahead
4. d

Giving Instructions

1. d
2. stop crying
3. 1d 2e 3a 4b 5c
4. c

Giving and Taking Advice

1. c
2. Why don't you tell him?
3. Wouldn't it be better if you calmed down a bit?
4. b

Nobody is Perfect

1. d
2. I'm sorry to bring this up
3. Look, I'm sorry to trouble you but . . .
4. b

Being Astonished, Being Surprised

1. d
2. Are you serious?
3. 1d 2e 3a 4c 5b
4. Really? Is that so?

Showing Doubt and Uncertainty

1. I haven't the slightest idea
2. 1d 2a 3b 4c 5e
3. I presume
4. b

Showing Likes and Preferences

1. b
2. 'd rather you didn't
3. 1d 2e 3a 4b 5c
4. How did you enjoy . . . ?/Marvellous!
5. d

We Are not Pleased

1. c
2. I hate
3. 1c 2a 3b 4e 5d
4. hate
5. c

Englisch

Englisch von Anfang an. Ein Sprachkurs zur wichtigsten Weltsprache, nach dem Alltag, orientiert am britischen und amerikanischen Sprachgebrauch.

U. Kreisel / P. A. Tabbert
English One *Englisch reden und verstehen. Ein Grundkurs*
(rororo sachbuch 9180)
English One *Toncassette*
(rororo sachbuch 9181)

Gunther Bischoff
Speak you English?
Programmierte Übung zum Verlernen typisch deutscher Englischfehler
(rororo sachbuch 6857)
Better Times *Ein leichtes Programm zum richtigen Gebrauch der englischen Zeiten*
(rororo sachbuch 7987)
Managing Manager English
Gekonnt verhandeln lernen durch Üben an Fallstudien.
(rororo sachbuch 7129)

René Bosewitz / Robert Kleinschroth
Joke by joke to Conversation
Sprechsituationen mit Witz gemeistert
(rororo sachbuch 8797)
Joke your Way through English Grammar *Wichtige Regeln zum Anlachen*
(rororo sachbuch 8527)

Hartmut Breitkreuz /René Bosewitz
Do up your Phrasals *500 Wendungen wichtiger Verben*
(rororo sachbuch 8344)
Getting on Top of Idiomatic Verbs
Tausend Wendungen im Kontext
(rororo sachbuch 8523)

3450/1

rororo sprachen

Hartmut Breitkreuz
More False Friends *Tückische Fallen des deutsch-englischen Wortschatzes*
(rororo sachbuch 9172)
False Friends *Stolpersteine des deutsch-englischen Wortschatzes*
(rororo sachbuch 8492)

Ernest Pasakarnis
Grammar Questions from A - Z
Everything you always wanted to know about Grammar but were afraid to ask
(rororo sachbuch 8491)
Master your Idioms *Der Schlüssel zu englischen Redewendungen*
(rororo sachbuch 8491)
The Word Lover^s Guide to How Words Work *Ein moderner Vokabeltrainer*
(rororo sachbuch 8426)
Those Pesky Prepositions! *Der heikle Umgang mit Präpositionen*
(rororo sachbuch 8785)

Emer O'Sullivan / Dietmar Rösler
Modern Talking *Englisches Quasselbuch mit Sprüchen und Widersprüchen*
(rororo sachbuch 8427)

Französisch

Französisch von Anfang an. Ein Sprachkurs nah an der Umgangssprache und dem französischen Alltag.

Armelle Damblemont / Petra Preßmar
Français Un *Französisch reden und verstehen. Ein Grundkurs*
(rororo sachbuch 9106)

Français Un *Toncassette*
Zum Auffrischen, Vertiefen und Ergänzen für mehr oder minder Sprachgewandte
(rororo sachbuch 9107)

Claire Bretécher / Isabelle Jue/ Nicole Zimmermannn
Le Français avec les Frustrés *Ein Comic-Sprachhelfer*
(rororo sachbuch 8423)
Plus de Français avec les Frustrés
Ein Comic-Srachhelfer
(rororo sachbuch 8539)

Ahmed Haddedou
Questions grammaticales de A à Z
Tout ce que vous avez toujours voulu savoir sur la grammaire sans jamais oser le demander
(rororo sachbuch 8445)

Robert Kleinschroth
La Conversation en s'amusant
Sprechsituationen mit Witz gemeistert
(rororo sachbuch 8873)

Robert Kleinschroth / Dieter Maupel
La Grammaire en s'amusant
Wichige Regeln zum Anlachen
(rororo sachbuch 8714)

rororo sprachen

Marie-Thérèse Pignolo / Hans-Georg Heuber
Ne mâche pas tes mots *Nimm kein Blatt vor den Mund! Französische Redewendungen und ihre deutschen Pendants*
(rororo sachbuch 7472)

Jacques Soussan
Pouvez-vous Français?
Programm zum Verlernen typisch deutscher Französischfehler
(rororo sachbuch 6940)

rororo sprachen wird herausgegeben von Ludwig Moos. Das Gesamtverzeichnis der Reihe finden Sie in der *Rowohlt Revue*. Jedes Vierteljahr neu. Kostenlos in Ihrer